# *Praise for* Hidden Treasure

"Gangaji is one of the smartest, clearest, and most poetic spiritual leaders of our time. Her writing in *Hidden Treasure* is compassionate, transparent, generous, and ruthless. The mere reading of only a few of her words brings me home in seconds to the truth of who I am."

—*Alanis Morissette, Grammy Award–winning singer and songwriter*

"To liberate oneself from the story of the ego is a momentous leap utterly necessary in order to wake up to your true nature. It is the transmission and tools for this great liberation from the story of ego that Gangaji gives her students and all of her readers. What a joy to feel the power of this liberation both in Gangaji's words and, even more, in the space of silence between the words. It is only from this place of liberation that resplendent glory of the unique perspective of your enlightenment can emerge in its full radiance. It is an honor and a delight to recommend this book to any sincere seeker."

—*Rabbi Marc Gafni, Ph.D., author of* Soul Prints *and* The Mystery of Love

"Gangaji's luminous words reflect her luminous Heart, which shines through in the naked telling of her story and her realization. There's a simplicity, beauty, and grace in her presence and her prose that comes from the real freedom underneath. Listen, absorb, relax, and know that you are already Home."

—*Stephen Dinan, CEO, The Shift Network, and author of* Radical Spirit

"We each have our own story of the life that we think we are living. But underneath this story lies the deeper truth of who we are—our real nature—and a life that is fully present. With simplicity, clarity, and the deep wisdom gained from her own lived experience, Gangaji gives us the tools we need to make this step into our real self. *Hidden Treasure* is an invitation to wake up into the truth and freedom that are always here."

—*Llewellyn Vaughan-Lee, Ph.D., Sufi teacher and author of*
The Return of the Feminine and the World Soul

"*Hidden Treasure* not only speaks to the transformation of consciousness, but is a tool for directly transforming consciousness. I turned the last page and felt cleansed, renewed. Ordinary things were more vividly imbued with the sacred, loved ones more lovable, the path home to my true being ample and gracious. The perennial truths Gangaji shares in this sublime book penetrate to the heart of our deepest longings, and reveal the treasures hidden in the places we have been conditioned to turn away from: the open fields of silence behind our stories."

—*Mirabai Starr, author of translations of* Dark Night of the Soul *and*
The Interior Castle, *both Riverhead books, part of the Penguin Group*

"What I love about *Hidden Treasure* is Gangaji's frankness and openness about her own journey, and her demonstrating how the very human challenges that mark our daily lives not only are inseparable from nondual realization, but are the means by which we travel to the core of our innermost self. Her guidance for inquiry is wise, helpful, and practical, and offered from a woman who has labored with love on the path of spirit and of life."

—*Mariana Caplan, Ph.D., author of* The Guru Question: The Perils and Rewards of Choosing a Spiritual Teacher *and* Eyes Wide Open: Cultivating Discernment on the Spiritual Path

# Hidden Treasure

# Hidden Treasure

UNCOVERING THE TRUTH
IN YOUR LIFE STORY

## Gangaji

JEREMY P. TARCHER/PENGUIN
a member of Penguin Group (USA) Inc.
New York

JEREMY P. TARCHER/PENGUIN
Published by the Penguin Group
Penguin Group (USA) Inc., 375 Hudson Street, New York, New York 10014, USA •
Penguin Group (Canada), 90 Eglinton Avenue East, Suite 700, Toronto, Ontario
M4P 2Y3, Canada (a division of Pearson Penguin Canada Inc.) • Penguin Books Ltd,
80 Strand, London WC2R 0RL, England • Penguin Ireland, 25 St Stephen's Green,
Dublin 2, Ireland (a division of Penguin Books Ltd) • Penguin Group (Australia),
250 Camberwell Road, Camberwell, Victoria 3124, Australia (a division of Pearson
Australia Group Pty Ltd) • Penguin Books India Pvt Ltd, 11 Community Centre,
Panchsheel Park, New Delhi–110 017, India • Penguin Group (NZ), 67 Apollo Drive,
Rosedale, North Shore 0632, New Zealand (a division of Pearson New Zealand Ltd) •
Penguin Books (South Africa) (Pty) Ltd, 24 Sturdee Avenue, Rosebank, Johannesburg
2196, South Africa

Penguin Books Ltd, Registered Offices: 80 Strand, London WC2R 0RL, England

First trade paperback edition 2012
Copyright © 2011 by Gangaji

Most Tarcher/Penguin books are available at special quantity discounts for bulk pur-
chase for sales promotions, premiums, fund-raising, and educational needs. Special
books or book excerpts also can be created to fit specific needs. For details, write Penguin Group (USA) Inc. Special Markets, 375 Hudson Street, New York, NY 10014.

The Library of Congress catalogued the hardcover edition as follows:

Gangaji.
  Hidden treasure : uncovering the truth in your life story / Gangaji.
    p.      cm.
  ISBN 978-1-58542-887-8
1. Self-realization.  2. Happiness.  3. Spiritual life.  I. Title.
  BF637.S4G348    2011
  204'.44—dc22              2011013625

ISBN 978-0-399-16053-0 (paperback edition)

Printed in the United States of America
10  9  8  7  6  5  4  3  2  1

BOOK DESIGN BY NICOLE LAROCHE

While the author has made every effort to provide accurate telephone numbers and
Internet addresses at the time of publication, neither the publisher nor the author
assumes any responsibility for errors, or for changes that occur after publication. Further, the publisher does not have any control over and does not assume any responsibility
for author or third-party websites or their content.

*Penguin is committed to publishing works of quality and integrity.
In that spirit, we are proud to offer this book to our readers;
however, the story, the experiences, and the words
are the author's alone.*

For my daughter, Sarah

# CONTENTS

# Part Three

# Introduction

My teacher told many teaching stories. Sometimes he told about a lion raised as a donkey who, through the good grace of another lion pointing out his inherent lion-ness to him, wakes up to his true nature and roars. Another time it would be the story of the exquisite hiding place in a thief's own pocket, where a rich merchant makes sure his brilliant diamond is secure. He often told the teaching story "Hidden Treasure" that sets the context for this book. In "Hidden Treasure," a grieving and humbled widow and her children discover that there had been a treasure under their feet the whole time they experienced poverty.

All of these stories teach us that we aren't who we think we are. How we have defined ourselves is not the truth of ourselves. What we think we must have is already present, and when we think we have lost the value of our lives, it is still here if we know where to look.

This book is offered as support in discovering that our individual stories can point to what is under our noses, even if we experience it as absent. We each have the capacity to discover the truth of who we really are, whatever our particular story may be.

We can find the treasure in our own being that we may think we have to look for somewhere else. And we can discover that no matter how the events of our lives are arranged and rearranged, true and lasting value is here, precisely where we stand.

This book is designed to demonstrate both how we keep ourselves in the dark and how—with nothing changing in our story—we can discover the light. The truth is simple, but the ways of obscuring the truth are complex. If we can simplify the complexities of our individual suffering, we are already closer to truth. We think we suffer uniquely, and our particulars may be somewhat unique, but the patterns are the same. In particular ways we are under the spell of ignorance. Ignorance can be described, and through this description it can be dispelled.

This book invites you to tell your story within the context of recognizing the peace and fulfillment that are always present in the core of your being. The book's purpose is to support you in seeing what gets in the way of that recognition—the "clothing" you have put on to cover the naked core of yourself. This covering is fabricated from the memory of past events—both your individual past and our collective, human past.

If you are like most humans, you are weaving fabric for this clothing in the present as you prepare story lines for the future.

# Introduction

If you are willing to stop weaving for a period of deep and truthful inquiry, you can discover what the stories cloak. In this book you are not asked to transcend your story. We can recognize the power and beauty and horror of particular stories, while also recognizing the necessity to see *through* these stories to discover what lives at the core.

In our long human history of storytelling, there have been great beings with awe-inspiring stories that reveal the victory of self-discovery. What inspires us about these great ones is that somehow their lives turned toward and then reflected the sublime discovery of everlasting truth. This book invites you to let your story be a contribution to the universal revelation of self-discovery, expressed uniquely as you.

This invitation is not as outrageous as it may initially appear. Even the greatest saints and realized beings had much that was ordinary in their life stories. They had pain and failure. Like us, they knew self-doubt and setbacks. When we are willing to recognize what was ordinary about those people, we can more fully embrace the possibility of our own lives turning toward and then reflecting direct and endless discovery of ourselves.

In this book you are asked to see underneath and inside the story. We have learned how to present ourselves, carefully covered for both protection and deception. To the degree that we are unaware of what is free inside us—regardless of our presentations—we suffer. As you either peel the layers off your story, or see through these layers, you stand naked to yourself, in silent awareness.

The thought of being naked to oneself can generate fear. Most of us are aware that we have a multitude of flaws, and to be fully naked brings with it the possibility of discovering yet more. We have both skillfully and unconsciously learned to cover our perceived flaws with layer upon layer of storytelling. Our internal images and narratives are only made of pictures and thoughts, but they wield mighty power. We may know them to be at least in part untrue, but most likely we fear that what is covered needs to be covered.

We have become practiced at maintaining the threads of our overlapping story lines, and we work to cover the unraveling holes that life persistently reveals. This is steady work, requiring our attention day and night. In an instant, if only for an instant, we can stop. When we are exhausted with our labor of covering what we fear we are, we can stop covering. When we are curious about what is unchanging in the midst of constant change, we can stop giving all our attention to what changes. When we are called to a life beyond our imagination, beyond our ability to construct, we can stop constructing our life. It is at this point that we discover that any thought of ourselves is only a thread that contributes to the weaving of a story, and that thread can be released. In this release we find the strength to view ourselves without covering. Our attention can return to the silent, aware core.

Silent, conscious awareness is naturally naked of phenomena and is nakedly present in the core of all phenomena. It is only our distraction with phenomena—"clothing" made of thoughts, images, sense impressions, and memory—that keeps our core cloaked from recognition.

By inquiring into your life story, you can recognize the layers of ephemeral distraction that keep your attention busy with entanglements. When you recognize them, you can reclaim your attention. You can allow the distractions to fall away, or you can see through them all the way home, to the silent core.

**In the first part** of this book, I present my own story and introduce "Hidden Treasure," the teaching story my teacher H. W. L. Poonja (Papaji) sometimes used. In the second part, these two stories are deconstructed, or "undressed." The purpose of this is to support you in deeper examination of your own life story. To more fully examine your story, you *undress* it. You see *inside* it. The book's continuing deconstruction of my story and the teaching story is support for the continuing deconstruction of your story.

When the essential insubstantiality of all that has been woven by thought is recognized, the cloaking device is exposed. You are naked. You can see the core of yourself, not as another object constructed by thought, but as the hidden treasure of the truth of yourself. Silent, aware consciousness is conscious of itself as eternal subject, eternal source—the naked core in your story, in my story, in the teaching story, and in all the infinite, mysterious variety of human stories.

Recognition of this is the completion of a life's search for fulfillment.

# Part One

# CHAPTER 1

# Stories

Most of my life was spent at war with the characters— including the lead, me—in my story. They weren't good enough, or smart enough, or deep enough. At one point in the story of me, none of us was rich enough. At another point, when material possessions were disdained, none of us was poor enough. It was never right. It could always be better. Sometime in the future, I could make my story turn out to fit my latest idealization, or so I hoped. For four decades I worked at building a story that would fulfill me. Periods of happiness and peace came and went. *Lasting* happiness remained out of my grasp. It took some time to realize that the lasting fulfillment I was seeking couldn't be captured by any story I told about myself. The fulfillment I was seeking in my many attempts to tell a story of victory couldn't be captured, because it is free. It took more time to realize that my story was mysteriously appearing in that which is already fulfilled. It was a beautiful and wonderful shock to discover that freedom and fulfillment were never absent, whatever the latest rendition of my story. My story was an individual display of the search for the living free consciousness already inhabiting each character. When I recognized the silent fulfilled core in all versions of myself—and all the others in my story—I could rest. In the spaciousness of rest, I could begin to live my life from fulfillment, rather than continuing to search for it.

All creatures are born inescapably defined by their stories, yet if we remain limited by those definitions we live a life of inner bondage. When we recognize the stories that generate our definitions of ourselves, we are closer to the discovery of what is indefinable within us. That discovery reveals inner freedom and lasting fulfillment.

Each life-form has a beginning, an arc of a life story, and then an ending. Most of our internal and external attention and communication circle around the particulars of how we define ourselves as collective life and how we define ourselves, or others, as particular life. Other animals, trees, flowers, butterflies, spiders, rocks, planets, and solar systems also have their stories, and the broadcasting of their stories is both our greatest entertainment and our inevitable humbling. We can find ourselves, or parts of ourselves, in all stories and we can separate ourselves through our stories.

We all come from life-giving energy, are infused and animated by life energy to become a particular life-form, and we all end in returning to formless life. Along the way there are small and great dramas, crossroads of destiny, and surprises both wondrous and horrific. Some life stories end very quickly and some go on and on. There are countless dramas within this bigger, incomprehensible universal story. Stories are sung, put into sacred books, memorized, dramatized, and consulted generation after generation. Our collective cosmic story is a teeming theater of life-forms appearing and disappearing. Forms are born, live through many stories, and then die. Before any form appears, life is here. During the lifetime of any form, life is animating that form. After any particular form dies, life—while withdrawn from that form—remains here. Life is true. It is always here.

Our particular, individual life story begins in our mother's womb. We are well- or ill-tended there through a number of convergent factors. While the incubation in the womb happens more or less the same for all humans, research has shown that the outside environment can also greatly affect the fetus. Whatever stories parents are living influence their developing baby. The diversity of womb environments ranges from the worst—babies conceived in concentration camps or prisons, babies born of rape, fetuses whose mothers are in dire poverty, crack babies, babies with fetal alcohol syndrome, fetuses whose mothers are mentally or physically ill—to the best: babies prenatally tended with love and care, in nontoxic physical, mental, and emotional environments for both fetus and mother. Genes and early environment contribute in great degree to form the earliest version of each individual creature's story, and yet even in the womb the early individual can mysteriously defy both best and worst.

We inherit much of the foundation for our story from our families and our communities of birth. We also have the innate ability as an intelligent life-form to consciously cast off much of what has been preordained for us or has previously defined us. Even something as seemingly fixed as gender is subject to cultural input for its meaning, and in our current era, through surgery and biomedicine, choice is possible. Our definitions of ourselves are formed, disassembled, and re-formed by what we absorb and what we reject.

The journey of a human life in even a day, and noticeably in a year, a decade, or a century, is a series of stories, a few relatively stabilized at the center, some contradictory, some similar, some long forgotten, and all manipulated and re-formed by the latest acceptance or rejection. We have a huge closet filled with the basic "clothing" of past events that we then rearrange, remix, or discard for particular needs at particular times. We have within our cells uncountable narratives of love and hate, of peace and war, of realized dreams and abject failures. Each plays its conscious and subconscious role in how we define and clothe ourselves. Each is a rendition or an aspect of the life story.

Since the definitions that are generated by our stories are stable only in part, inquiring into our stories—especially their central themes—can reveal early and continuing arrangements of events to support a particular central identity. Definitions of who we are as individuals are changeable and are rearranged to be worn for the latest version or role being played in our particular story, but the central identity is what we refer to when we say "I" or "me." It is what finally feels solid to us as the changing winds of success and failure swirl through our thoughts.

When our parents are in charge of our lives, they have the greatest input into our developing identities. By the time we begin school, we are open and available for the input of our peers and we grow into more socially formatted identities. When adolescence hits, our hormonal imperative reveals that we are no longer who we thought we were even a few years earlier. As our individuation dynamically continues, the central identity continues to apparently solidify. Maturation and then old age, with their accompanying biological and cultural stories, prove that while our individual "me" may feel solid, the periphery is always changing.

The truth of our stories is not bound to the verifiable facts of the story. Shakespeare's version of Richard III may be only loosely factual, but the character in the play vibrates with an aspect of human character. The memories you have may be in complete accord with your character and the thrust of your life without having much to do with the actual events around those memories. Memories are fabricated in many ways—through others' stories, through fears and desires, through neurosis or psychosis, or just through the small adaptations added with growing perspective. In a real sense the events in our memory are fluid. They flow around, crash into, or adapt themselves to our latest versions of ourselves.

The facts themselves are not even true, if by *true* we mean that which remains unchanging. The so-called facts are assumed to be of central importance at one time and irrelevant at another. They come and go at our convenience. At any one time the facts of our life may reflect the truth of our life, but this reflection is always at least slightly warped. The very vastness of life remains free of our objectification of it.

The recognition that nothing that can be recaptured in memory is verifiable as actual truth is both humbling and liberating. When we meet with friends and family, as well as enemies, and recollect the past, it can be shocking to discover how events have been created or forgotten. Of course, our memory of particular events may seem irrefutable to us. To others, with opposing memories of those same events, the same irrefutability is just as certain. We believe our mental/emotional objectification of events—our stories—even when actual factual evidence to the contrary is presented to us.

There are many who live torturous lives of unremitting toil and suffering. There are also many who live lives filled with miserable events and yet mysteriously do not suffer. And, just as mysterious, there are those who live lives of ease and plenty and yet suffer greatly. Our inner lives are certainly affected by external facts, but they are not controlled by those facts. The truth of one's life, whether a life of suffering or a life of ease, does not lie in the *facts* of that life. Our inquiry here is concerned with the truth of your life. The events, and memories of those events, are the clothes that can obscure the naked truth of your life. The events, and the assemblage of memories around those events, of a life story can be the starting point of the disrobing into that inner truth.

When we recognize the unreliability of memory, we become liberated from the practice of looking into it for definitions and proofs of who we are. Our attention is then free to discover the unchanging truth of ourselves, our deepest inner life. The mental and emotional energy we expend telling and retelling our stories internally in our thought dialogues and externally in our presentations of ourselves can be shifted. We can direct our attention to discovering what is unaltered regardless of infinite alteration all around. We can turn our attention toward the truth of the matter rather that the definition of the matter.

The interaction and overlapping of one's story and another's story happens throughout our lives. Our family's story, our clan's story, our racial story, our religious or nonreligious story, our national story, and the multitude of other stories we find ourselves a part of are woven of the threads of narratives. Our personal story is another thread, a part of many greater weavings. The importance of the influence of others on us and us on others cannot be overemphasized.

It is natural in our species for families, nations, religions, cultures, and subcultures to pass on knowledge through storytelling. This book is concerned primarily with the spoken and written word, but stories are universally transmitted in prose or poetry, music, dance, and art of every medium. From our earliest learning and throughout our lives, we look to stories to show us the way. And they do. For better and worse, our stories become the reference points for defining who we are, who we are with, and what it all means.

Most likely our first stories are sung to us when we are infants. A favorite memory of mine is bouncing on my daddy's knee to a song about a horse. When the part came about the "horsey falling down," his knee would collapse and I would fall to the floor, except that he still held me by the hands. I would squeal in pleasure and excitement as we played it over and over. Perhaps the primary nourishment of the game was feeling my father's love, but it was also an essential lesson about things collapsing and remaining all right in the midst of that collapse. It was an introduction to the surprises of the world, cushioned by the support of a primary protector.

As we grow older, if we are lucky we have stories read to us. A children's story is usually framed in the context of teaching the values and taboos of the child's culture. To more easily grab the attention of the child's mind they are designed to thrill and frighten. Often the endings are reassuring. Cinderella does get the Prince even though she had to go through the suffering of being unseen and misunderstood before her victory. Often they are terrifying. Little Red Riding Hood learns a lesson of the dangers of naively believing in appearances, even though she too is saved in the end. The context of most archetypical children's stories is the preparation of children for the dangers of the world. It is a noble and necessary task for each generation. There are also more subtle children's stories that address the inner world and the mysteries of the universe. These stories acknowledge the hugeness of a child's surroundings and help somewhat in navigation. In these more inward-directed stories, the context is also teaching and guidance along with supporting and soothing.

If we are lucky we learn to read and can begin to choose what stories to fold into our identity. I discovered reading to myself at an early age, and it has remained an essential aspect of my life since. The stories and books I read entertained me and gave me an escape from aspects of life out of my control. I would try to be more like the characters I loved, Heidi and later Nancy Drew, and would revel in their successes over the inevitable trials in their path. My storybook characters contributed greatly to the formation of myself as a person. Later, in more mature reading, I began to discover subtleties and nuances of character that would deepen my experiences of others and myself. Stories guided me into deeper waters. Stories helped me formulate and define myself. They served as both solace and challenge.

A story that teaches by design can either be pedantic, and therefore most usually off-putting, or subtle and penetrating. A sublime teaching story enters the mind stream almost before the intellect has realized its meaning. We can be caught up in following the story line, while the story line is already changing our perception of reality. Those are the best, and we have those passed down to us throughout the ages. They are the holy books of all religions, the epics of each culture, and the folktales and nursery rhymes that live through word of mouth without even the need of literacy.

When we evoke the stories of such different world characters as Christ, the Buddha, Harriet Tubman, Ulysses, Wonder Woman, Harry Potter, and any other hero of any type, the story changes our state of mind and our physiology. When we follow the arcs of their lives we see a mirror of the blessings and curses of our own lives. We gather nourishment and learn essential warnings from the narratives of their lives.

We can follow Christ's life and personally relate to his adolescent awakening to the power to throw off corrupted authority. If we later learn that this version of Christ's life was fabricated as early Christian propaganda by a zealous disciple called Paul, we nevertheless irrationally remain inspired. It is not in the *facts* but in the truth of adolescent individuation that his story is now our story, and it emboldens us to throw off the perceived corruptions of our parents to find our own way. We can emotionally relate to the betrayal by his disciple, as we weep over our own betrayals and betrayings. We suffer his crucifixion as we recognize we are unseen by our society and peers. We rejoice in his ascension as we take heart in our own capacity for renewal and new beginnings.

From stories about the Buddha and Harriet Tubman we discover how a previously sheltered prince and a hardy slave both found the fortitude needed to escape their radically different imprisonments to answer the call of freedom. We see in their life stories extremely individual ways of serving others. The Buddha uses his profound insight to point to the peace accompanying nonattachment. Harriet Tubman personifies the resolve necessary for attaining physical freedom and assisting others in attaining the same. Though their stories are fundamentally different from each other, each points us to revelation and fortitude available in our own story.

With Ulysses we see how easily even the strongest intentions of our conscious wills can be led astray by siren songs of all kinds. With Wonder Woman or Harry Potter we feel the thrill of the possibility that the mystery of life can be channeled through our personal power, and regardless of our mistakes and humanness, we too can discover and live up to our talents.

All stories show us facets of ourselves waiting to be revealed. If we assume that our personal heroes show us our own favored identities and emerging inner qualities, we can also see that villains and minor characters likewise reveal aspects of ourselves. The most indelible stories endure throughout the centuries because they reveal to us that we are wise and good as well as ignorant and villainous.

We are inspired and cautioned by stories. We learn something about our relationship to time by hearing our mother read *The Poky Little Puppy* enough times. We realize the great follies of our vanity and misused power from the universal epics. From Shakespeare, Homer, and Faulkner we learn what failure is, what perseverance means, how the choice of an instant can doom or save a person's or a nation's life. Science fiction stories reveal that the choice of an instant can even threaten all life-forms.

We are entertained by stories in movies and books, in gossip and in scripture. Stories are the vehicle and proof of the power of language. They are the central jewel in the crown of language.

We are manipulated by the stories we hear over and over, as well as the stories we read and reread, and tell and retell. Mostly we are swept along with the prevailing cultural or subcultural stories and their definitions of who we are both as a group and as individuals. We may believe the latest reasons for war, the necessity of working more even with less reward, and the approaching apocalyptic end of the world, or we may be in rebellion against these typical and current cultural story lines. Either way, it is the predominant cultural narrative that forms the polarity of reference points. We may study the ways of propaganda in our schoolrooms, but the subtlety of the cultural story often leaves us blind to our personal contribution to and entanglement in that group narrative.

What we are often mostly unaware of, as we absorb the stories around us, is the structure and message of the story we are living. More often we use the stories of our past and present cultural heritage to avoid fully recognizing the story that lives through us. We may be aware of our particular triumphs or miseries, but we rarely have a perspective or overview of how our story has served to define us. If the story is in a phase of failure, we usually accept the definition that we are failures. If the story turns toward success, then we are successes, although perhaps haunted by the earlier definition of failure. We may be telling ourselves of our success and fearing failure, but normally we do not recognize the possibility of not being defined by any particular story line. We are less free to the degree that we consciously or unconsciously accept these definitions.

How can we live lives, which most certainly are stories, and yet not be defined by these stories? We can be free *in* the story of ourselves; we can live free of any definition of ourselves. That freedom rests on the recognition of the nature of change and changelessness. Usually we either long for or fear change. And change is the nature of any story. Lasting freedom and fulfillment are only found in changelessness. The changeless is the conscious, silent awareness that is present regardless of any turn of events, regardless of any clothing. If we overlook changeless, silent awareness, we overlook that which is already free of all bondage, free of any *definition* of freedom.

Rather than focusing our attention and judgment on change as the *obstacle* to recognizing the changeless, we can use our stories and their changing events as catalysts to reveal the changeless substratum. We begin with stories and the definitions they generate so that we can use the discomfort that often accompanies them to evoke true questioning. True questioning pulls our attention deeper into ourselves, under the story lines and definitions into the core.

In seemingly mysterious and sometimes unwanted ways, our particular story is also expressing exactly what we need to face if we want to deepen our experience of life. When we recognize what the essential thrust of our life reveals, we can begin to see how the present rendition of our story also offers the essential wisdom needed to evolve into the next phase. Our stories are often ruthless in their insistence on particular lessons. When we are willing to remove the judgments of particular aspects of our story, even if those judgments are legitimate, we have the opportunity to learn in a fresh and unexpected way. In that learning we are unhindered by definitions of right or wrong, even though right and wrong may have been essential elements to the story.

Stepping back and viewing your story from a larger perspective can at least disengage your entanglement with your story. Personally, at a certain point of oversaturation with my own story, I had to stop formulating and believing my story's narrative. I had to at least take a break from myself! In that break I realized what a mess I was continuing to generate by how I defined myself and others. I could learn from my mistakes and start afresh, but first I had to stop crying. The crying stops instantly when there is no story to evoke it.

This fresh moment was available for me to discover how to live with more integrity and with more kindness, but finally its essential teaching was that to discover anything freshly, all definitions of what is known have to be released.

All of history is the record of alliances and conflicts with one another's stories. Our human history is proof of both the fragility and final unreliability of definitions we have lived under. Enemies become allies and then enemies again within a decade. Empires explode and implode, loving marriages dissolve in divorce, religions of peace become excuses for war. Our human history also points to what prevails regardless of our follies and complicities in horror. Conscious, aware life is still here. In you and in others, regardless of construction or destruction, life remains.

"The Emperor's New Clothes" is a pertinent teaching story for discovering our own nakedness. In this old tale, the emperor was swindled by some famous tailors to believe that he wore a suit of clothes so refined that only those of superior intelligence and worth would be able to see it. Of course he didn't see any suit of clothes, as it did not exist, but since he didn't want to appear lacking in intelligence and worth, he pretended to see it. In his pretense, he marveled at the beauty that would cover him and made plans for a parade among his subjects. Word got out about these refined clothes that could only be seen by the best of people, and people everywhere marveled to each other over the emperor's new clothes as he paraded naked through the town. Only a small child, unaware of the consequences of being judged an inferior person, dared to call out, "The emperor is naked!" The emperor flinched, as somewhere deep inside he knew himself to be naked, but he covered his reaction quickly and continued his glorious parade in his gloriously nonexistent clothing.

If we are able to recognize the stories we weave, and recognize that they have no real substance, then we are closer to the innocent truth of ourselves. We can recognize the trance of being caught in belief that the story of the thing is the truth of that thing. We can recognize that even the grandest story is subject to unraveling. We can be willing to follow the discomfort of our inner flinch into the truth of our nakedness.

At this time in our present history we have the ability to be conscious of the stories we have been taught and how they define us, as well as the stories we have unquestionably believed about who another is. We can be willing to be naked to ourselves, and we can take responsibility for the result. We can marvel when we discover that the stories of previously demonized others (enemies) are as beautiful and multilayered as our own. We mature when we realize that some of the stories cherished as the foundation of our culture are flimsy and insubstantial in truth and are sometimes outrightly false. One generation's true and defining story can be proved to be a lie in the next generation. Stories that celebrate freedom and revolution against tyranny can turn on themselves and become stories of reigns of terror.

We recognize the location of the story in our flesh and emotions. From this recognition choice is born. We have most often either chosen to continue the given story or to rebel against that story. Naturally we have been thrilled to realize that we can choose to live a different story, one we feel more in alignment with. There is yet another choice. We have the capacity to take a moment and *release all* stories. We can experience what it means to be nobody, uncovered even by our primary identity.

Underneath all the stories, we can experience that deep core of ourselves that is historyless, genderless, and parentless. Naked. That presence is unencumbered by relationships and has no past and no future. In the core of our beingness we are free of

definitions. Unencumbered by our definitions, we experience ourselves as conscious intelligence aware of itself as open, endless
space. This instant of being storyless is an instant of freedom. For
even if our story is filled with light and beauty, to the degree that
we define ourselves through that story, we are less free.

After such a moment, stories are never the same. They can be
present, as they most likely will be, but they no longer have the
inherent power to define our reality. The inner wealth that is
available to us is no longer limited or augmented by particular
inner or outer events. While the personality or the "creatureness"
of each individual continues just as stories continue, the underlying awareness, the true "I," has come home to itself.

After such a moment, choice is present, where we were blindly
choiceless before. When we are not blinded by the stories that
have been created for us, or the stories we create, we can appreciate the mysterious vastness that is holographically present in
each moment of any story. We can discover what is and has
always been here, throughout whatever rendition of story was
being lived or believed. Each of us can take any story from our
past, and we can discover the treasure that was hidden only
through unquestioning belief in narrowly focused assumptions
of the time. Stories can then be profoundly appreciated as displays of multidimensional life expressing itself in all forms.

What is the frame or context of your life? You don't know
how your story will end, but at this point you can discover what

your story is about. You can ask yourself how your inner sense of self is expressed, or has gone unexpressed, in the structure and message of your life story.

How does a particular success or failure fit into the whole of your life story? We tend to focus on and magnify particular events, but if we see them as part of a continuum, we can see the trajectory of the arc of our life story. Seeing in this way does not mean attempting to take control of the story. Instead, this is an invitation to tell the truth about what your story has been teaching so far. It is an invitation to recognize how your story fits into the larger context of what is important now to you as a human being. It is an invitation to discover how awareness and inquiry naturally broaden, deepen, and expand your own story so that it demonstrates precisely what needs to be learned. Since stories both archetypal and banal ultimately teach us something, investigate what your story teaches. Regardless of where you are in your story—still at the beginning, the hopefully long middle, or near the end—what bigger story does your life story contribute to?

Just becoming more aware of the stories we live, along with their infinite plotlines and subplots, begins to wake us up. In lucid dreaming, we become aware of ourselves as both in the dream story and outside it. In lucid living, as in lucid dreaming, we are no longer tyrannized by the stories circulating around and inside us. The demon in the nightmare can be faced directly; the flying dream can be enjoyed in its ecstatic moment. As we face ourselves in our stories, we have space for perspective. We can stand back and see our personal story as part of a bigger whole.

What is your story? You discover your story by noticing what you are telling yourself over and over. Notice what you tell yourself about your past, your present, and your future. In order to have any lasting impact, our stories have to be told and retold. All stories have a narrative. Your narrative is what you tell your-self through thoughts and images with accompanying emotions. What is your narrative? You can check right now. It is bound to be familiar. It is natural as human animals with developed cogni-tive abilities to generate and follow the narrative of our stories. It certainly is not wrong to do so. But it is limiting. It limits atten-tion to events that are forever changing. To discover how your attention is being spent, discover what you habitually say to your-self. Listen to your narrative while suspending belief in it.

There is great and mysterious power in knowing the potential gift of your life as a teaching story. This book is not written to teach you skills to create your version of reality. You are already doing that with your internal narrative. It is an invitation to be quiet and unidentified in the events that are appearing in and around your consciousness. In this quiet, there is a revelation impossible to discern if your attention is caught by the noise of identification.

The revelation does not bestow greater power to create a better story. It is bigger than that. Revelatory power can take the events of your life *as they are* and show them as essential to your own awakening as well as your contribution to the awakening of all humanity.

It is a power that shifts the story line from one limited to "about *me*" to one about *all*. With that shift there is both a profound surrender and a closer attention to how all is unfolding. There is paradoxically a disidentification with any character and a truer welcoming of all aspects of each character.

In profound, redemptive stories there is a moment of surrender to a deep command of being. This is not esoteric. It is concretely grounded in all who live fulfilled lives, however their fulfillment may be described. Whether it be religious, artistic, scientific, or ordinarily personal, there is recognition of something unarticulated by intellect. Surrender to this is surrender to the consciousness of being rather than to the conditioned structure of thought. With this deep and true surrender, stories shift in their perspective. With this shift you are no longer veiled from yourself. You are no longer bound by whatever inner or outer definitions may appear in your life story. All definitions and stories arise from the silent core, and in surrender all are then pointers to where they come from and where they return at their end. In surrender all is transparent from the luminosity of your naked self.

# CHAPTER 2

# My Story

## CLARKSDALE, MISSISSIPPI

When I was eleven or twelve, sitting on the curb in front of my house in the Mississippi summer heat, I knew I was waiting for something to happen. I didn't have faith that it would happen. I had more faith that I was trapped in a murky fate of punishment for some unknown crime. I only knew to sit there and hate the horror of being the victim of my birth, my family, my town, and—most of all—my own inner darkness.

From the outside, I really didn't have much to complain about. My family was poisoned by alcoholism, but my father provided for us. We three children had little to worry about externally. We had some status in the small town, and we always had enough food. We were free to wander around the town—the white people's section—and play on the banks of the local creek. In many ways, it was a good life.

But inside, I was falling apart. The way ahead seemed doomed to more of this hell. I could see that I was flawed and ugly and I felt there was no way out. I often indulged in this misery. So often that even though I never got to the bottom of it, I did get sick of it. I felt unloved, and I was sick of feeling unlovable. I felt unseen and I was sick of being unseen. I wanted love! I wanted to be seen! By some intelligence, I recognized that the more I wallowed in my misery, the more I felt unloved and unseen. I then made a conscious choice to get love and recognition.

At that time, in the mid-1950s, there was plenty of advice for young girls seeking love and attention. I found a series of books that taught me how to act, how to relate to other people, and how to look my best. I studied them with fervor every night. Soon I was smiling at people and remembering their names. It worked! People smiled back, and I felt more loved.

The more smiles exchanged, the more love I felt. Of course, smiles didn't always answer my smile, and when that happened I was once again face-to-face with my internal misery. However, success spurred me on, and the occasional setback effectively provided the reminder of what defeat would reveal.

I learned to please myself by pleasing others. I discovered that most everyone wanted to be pleased, so I worked at becoming pleasing. It was exhausting work. I developed insomnia, and nightmares came with the fitful sleep I did get. My body was always run-down, and I always feared I had some dire disease that would doom my work of being happy. My nervous system was on alert for signs of success or failure. But in spite of the nervous exhaustion, I was off the curb in front of my house. However much I felt the beast at my back, I was running ahead.

I became quite popular. In that popularity there was enough security to develop an authentic personality. I was far from a goody-goody. I was also brave enough to disagree when I did disagree, and I often broke the rules at school. I was wild enough to have many good times. And if I had to stagger the times a date would pick me up around my mother's drunkenness, well, I was having fun dating. I had good girlfriends, and with their love I no longer missed the perceived lack of my mother's love as much. I made good grades in school to please my daddy, and in the process I fell in love with learning. Mixed blessings, but most certainly a time of blessings. With no enlightenment and no inner reflection, it was only shallow pleasure but lots of it. I basked in it.


## OLE MISS


Then I went to college and had a rude awakening. The University of Mississippi (Ole Miss) was a beautiful, provincial university in 1960. It became deservedly infamous in 1962 for student riots against the freedom of an African-American to integrate the school, but in comparison with Clarksdale it was metropolitan. Hardly anyone knew me, and I wasn't pretty enough to attract attention. People more popular and more intelligent than I were everywhere. I was in a good sorority, I had friends, but I had lost my star power. My years of glory ended abruptly.

At the time, I hated the ending, but now I can see how lucky I was. I became disillusioned with my capabilities to create my happiness. This was a painful, deepening disillusionment. It opened my attention and energy to questions I never would have considered had my former success continued. Without realizing it at the time, the loss of my prior position paved the way for some of the most essential experiences of my life.

An unlikely friend from out of state was amused at my country ways while being horrified at the closed state of mind behind them. We had many stimulating conversations, different from any I had ever experienced. She questioned my unquestioned racism, my snobbery, and in general my insular mind. She introduced me to a professor of history who changed my life. She convinced me to enroll me in a religion class that acted as an earthquake to my orderly Episcopalian beliefs. I started to grow up.

Since I was not particularly popular, the maintenance of my persona took much less time. I used this time to experiment with broadening my worldview. I discovered that my inculcated racist beliefs were not fixed, and they began to fall away. I identified myself with a renegade group of quasi-bohemians I had met through my new friend. I began to revel in the freedom of anonymity, and I felt my new identity to be superior to the one I had mourned losing.

Then my heart got broken. I resisted his advances initially, but in a moment of alcohol-induced freedom I accepted. For a brief time I was happily in love. Then he moved on to the next conquest, and I was left with my inherently unlovable, ugly self. This was the next rung down into the hell I had experienced at the onset of puberty. I recognized that the advances I had made, whether social or intellectual, could never save me from the abyss that was my secret self. My insomnia returned, my striving to please began again, and I searched for a safe way to live my life.

To an eighteen-year-old young woman conditioned by the mores of the South of the early sixties, safety was in making a good marriage. With this in mind, I met a wonderful, intelligent boy who was studying medicine. Within a year we were in love and I wore his fraternity pin. We had a deep connection, and I felt sure he would save me. Life was simplified. When he left Ole Miss to attend medical school, I pursued my studies with vigor. My love of learning grew and I was deeply satisfied. Except sometimes, in the middle of the night, a desolate, sickening feeling would seep into my consciousness. Luckily, or so I thought at the time, I kept by my bed a small bottle of pills prescribed for me when I was just six years old. At that age I had experienced terrifying out-of-body sensations. The rational "cure" at the time for these phenomena was phenobarbital. I could take one of these pills and, blessedly, stop being haunted by my personal demons. I periodically used those pills from the time I was six until I was in my late twenties.

At this present time in my life I make no value judgment on the use of these pills. They helped me when there was no other help available. Medicine of all kinds has its place.

## MEMPHIS

After graduation from college, and a year of graduate studies, I had a huge and glorious wedding befitting marrying a man of such merit and status. Happily, expecting only the best, I settled into life as a medical student's wife. I taught junior and senior high school English and history. I waxed the floors of our sweet, modest apartment, and I ironed even his T-shirts as I waited for the right time to have a baby. Surely a baby would finalize my trajectory of security. Married life was a novelty, and I had high hopes of performing it so well that I would find final happiness.

Fairy tales don't come true, or at least not as we imagine. In my naiveté I continued to believe that if I could line up the right components, I would achieve a truly happy life. I did line them up. I had a good husband, the vitality of youth, and then a beautiful baby girl. The baby girl was the first shock wave in this perfect dream. She was an actual person, not just a fulfillment of narcissistic versions of myself. She interrupted my needs with her needs. She confirmed my latent belief that I was not good enough. I was failing as a mother. I imagined that she saw through me and recognized me for the fraud I was. A major chink appeared in my wall against the reality of life. As my dream of "perfect mother" was shattered by my incompetence, other areas of my dream life were exposed. The initial youthful passion I had felt for my husband disappeared, and I began faking it.

I faked it so well that I once again became exhausted and consumed by hypochondria. Once I even insisted that my husband hospitalize me for the flu just so I could get to the safety of the hospital bed, with no responsibilities of my own. What a mess! This time it was quite clear to me that I was the only one guilty of the mess. My daughter was bright and intelligent, and I loved her. My husband was happy and fulfilled in his work and home life, and I deeply respected and valued him. I was miserable and there was no one else to blame.

## SAN FRANCISCO

Finally the mess could no longer be maintained. When my daughter was four and we as a family had moved to San Francisco, I told my husband of my misery. He was rightfully shocked. In his innocence he had assumed all was well. We had arguments as all couples do, but that I was leaving the marriage was a hurtful surprise to him. I only felt that I had to escape, and I experienced great relief in finally being able to tell him, and myself, the truth. Immediately I was a better and more comfortable mother to my daughter, and a better friend to my soon to be ex-husband. I stopped living the lie of my life.

There was a new exuberance in my life. I was finished trying to live the way I had been told to live. I felt reborn. And reborn in San Francisco in 1972! New life was everywhere. Old ways of living by old rules and old ideas of happiness were discarded like old clothes. I was free to be with people different from any I had ever known. Since there were long waiting lists for would-be teachers, I took a job as a cocktail waitress and loved it. My daughter was in a cooperative preschool in North Beach, and the other parents were living lives I could never have dreamed of back on the curb in Mississippi.

We smoked pot and took mescaline and LSD. We called each other "brother" and "sister" and believed it. The spiritual world had more meaning and substance than the so-called real world. What a time! I tasted freedom. I recognized and experienced dimensions outside my previous, meager life. I meditated and chanted and went to see exotic gurus. It was wonderfully intoxicating. I wouldn't trade it for anything, and yet it too finally revealed itself to be inadequate in erasing the old demon of self-hatred.

After a few years and many experiences, I recognized that I was still lonely. I was still waiting for something I could not name. I had reveled in having many lovers after a monogamous and monotonous marriage. Now I felt emptied out and longed for a steady, true relationship. Once again, what I had achieved in my attempt to escape had proven to be empty. Once again I was stuck with myself.


## BOLINAS


My ex-husband had a house in Bolinas where our daughter lived and where he and I spent alternating parts of the week. It was a simple house, but Bolinas itself was dazzling in its natural beauty. The house was on the California cliffs above the Pacific Ocean and only a short walk to town and the beach. At that time the town was primarily a hippie and rancher town. The physical beauty was equally matched by the excitement and the mutual recognition of its inhabitants at their good luck. The good luck was in being in such a place and being with such an eclectic, talented group of people. There were dances, and drumming, and festivals. There were readings with famous, soon to be famous, and almost famous poets and writers. There were herb-gathering classes, health classes, and both a doctor and dentist who embraced alternative medicine. It was a place to grow, a place to experiment—a perfect place for me in this new phase of disillusionment.

My daughter was in an alternative child-centered school and had a wonderful, cranky old Shetland pony. When I was with her in Bolinas, I took photographs that would be critiqued in the photography classes I was taking in San Francisco. There were lots of portraits of my daughter and me. Now when I see them, I see the contrast between the two of us. There is a growing, beautiful, and fiery child, and then there is a lonely woman, displaying a despair she was only vaguely aware of.

What I was aware of was the lack of a male partner, and I began to dream of the perfect mate. This time he would be just right and would save me from a life of loneliness. Asking myself what I wanted, I imagined a tall, Nordic type. I would visualize my new family several times a day: my daughter, my new man, and our new baby. I was oblivious to the repetition of my earlier pattern of searching for rescue in exactly the same way. It seemed to me that this time was different, since I had changed so much through all the extreme experiences I had embraced. I didn't look or feel like the same person, except in the middle of some nights when the dark, ugly murkiness came to call.

Eli came into my life unexpectedly. He was nothing like my visualization of the perfect mate. He was younger and wilder than I was. He was swarthy rather than Nordic. He was not interested in marriage or even a committed relationship. He was extreme in his personality and offered no security at all. I fell profoundly in love with him. I felt myself open to realms that were irresistible. He was a force unknown to me, beyond any power of my imagination to visualize, and I surrendered to the love I felt.

Eli's primary interests were truth and freedom. For him to have any more than a passing interest in me, those had to be important to me too. I had mouthed the words "enlightenment," "peace," and "truth," but they really had been only the language of the lifestyle I was living. I liked the idea of enlightenment, and I tried to be a good person in spite of the badness I knew to be inside; but I had no notion of discipline or practice and no notion of what was required to recognize the demands of ego. I had recently started meditating for twenty minutes twice a day, but it was a miserable experience for me. I used a timer, but during my "meditation" I often checked to see if the timer was broken. How long twenty minutes could be!

I became Eli's student as well as his lover. He was studying tai chi, so I studied tai chi. He read Lao Tzu, so I did too. Pot became a holy sacrament, and we smoked it to open our hearts and expand our minds. Before Eli, pot had been like wine for me, just another pleasurable substance. We sat in silence for long periods; we talked in depth of the possibility of being free of our individual desires and serving all. We prepared great meals together, and, wonderfully, we laughed and laughed.

The years passed. When she was thirteen, my daughter went to Berkeley to be with her father and his new wife full time. After that, Eli and I moved to Mill Valley, and our footloose, magical Bolinas days came to an end.

## MILL VALLEY

It was time to reenter the regular world. By this time I had become a successful enough acupuncturist, and Eli was ready to establish a practice in neurolinguistics. We had stopped our arduous, fantastical Tibetan Buddhist practice and had become a California version of mainstream. I was happy. Eli and I still had some essential and crucial differences, but our partnership was alive with passion and companionship. My daughter was flourishing in her new environment, and we visited each other on weekends. Surprising to me, I discovered that this level of happiness was not enough.

No longer was I satisfied with achieving my lifelong goal of an extremely pleasurable life. Underneath the happiness and success, there was a deep yearning. It was different from my old cries for escape or for a man; this yearning had no formulation. It didn't have an object attached to it, but I felt it in my bone marrow. If I stayed busy, I could usually keep it below the surface of my conscious experience, and on trips to Maui, it lessened.

# MAUI

After living the good life in Mill Valley for seven years, we moved to Maui. Although we had continued to pursue spiritual goals by attending meditation retreats, reading works of living and dead masters, and discovering the power of the enneagram, we were exhausted by the demands of our materialistic lifestyle. We had always relaxed deeply while visiting Maui, and we felt that by moving there we would be more true to our deepest intentions of truth and peace. Thirteen years after first living together, and a year after moving to Maui, we resolved our essential differences about monogamy and married. A year later, Eli was internally called to the East to find a true teacher. While he was away, I allowed my inner yearning to rise to the surface, and I realized what I yearned for was to be free of myself, or what I thought was myself. I yearned to be free of my persistently recurring self-involvement.

While in India, through a miraculous series of events, Eli found himself at the door, and then the feet, of Sri H. W. L. Poonja, affectionately called Papaji. He wrote me letters of bliss and realization, and then he came back to get me to take me to this living master. Meeting this master was the ending of the life story I had known and lived. Meeting him finally revealed the consummation of my longing. After Papaji, nothing would ever be the same.

## HARIDWAR/LUCKNOW, INDIA

I had never desired to travel to India, and I had harsh judgments about the guru scene I had witnessed in the 1970s and 1980s in the United States. I had imagined the aesthetic surroundings of a Zen temple or the pristine beauty of Maui as the home of the answer to my mysterious yearning. But before Eli left on his search, we had both realized that our spiritual fulfillment required a true teacher. We knew that we had done what we could do on our own. We had prayed for a true teacher, and in my first meeting with Papaji, I saw that true teacher, and he lived in India.

His eyes, his smile, and his huge welcome embraced me to the marrow. In an instant I knew for certain I was exactly where I must be to discover what I must discover. When he asked me what I had come for, I answered, "Freedom."

He said, "Good. You are in the right place. Now do nothing, be still."

The next day Eli and I and four or five devotees from France met with him. I listened carefully as different people asked questions. He answered all in ways particular to the questioner, and his answers consistently and strongly pointed attention away from internal dialogue back into the endless space where all internal dialogue originates.

The room was warm and sticky with humidity, yet I strangely felt both elated and peaceful. There were odd sounds and strange smells coming from the street right below us, but the room was infused with luminosity. My body relaxed more and more, and after about an hour, I asked my question. "What do I need to do to be free?" He answered, "Stop. Stop everything. Then you will realize you are the freedom you have been searching for."

I was startled. Surely there was some esoteric practice I could do. Some way of getting rid of my ego? Some mystical incantation? Something? I had never considered "Stop." As I let his instruction seep into my consciousness over the next few days, different emotions appeared, primarily fear. When I didn't "go" with fear, it dissipated. In its place was, as best as I can describe it, a gentle spaciousness. Sometimes emotions and feelings I was familiar with, but had no easy category for, appeared. If I mentally fought with them or gave meaning to them, there were more thoughts to follow and more anguish. If I "stopped," the thoughts stopped and the feelings either moved on or disappeared.

One day Papaji asked, "Who are you?" and for an instant I knew with all certainty that I was the spaciousness that thoughts and emotions come from, the same spaciousness that remained when thoughts and emotions disappeared. The instant with its perfect knowing passed as I paid attention to the thought "This is it! Now I've got it!"

But the unwinding of identification with thoughts and emotions had begun.

After some weeks and many moments of beauty and grace as well as moments of terror and pain, it was time to return to Maui. Papaji had given me the name Gangaji, and he asked that I share my experience with those who were interested. I had no idea how this could happen, but he assured me that I didn't need an idea for it to all unfold effortlessly.

After leaving Haridwar and returning home, I began to write him at least daily. He answered many of my letters with thrilling confirmation and always inspiration for deeper inquiry. Then one night while I was with Eli as he led one of his groups at Esalen, a clap of thunder roared through my consciousness. In an instant all doubt of true identity disappeared. I laughed until I cried. We called Papaji the next morning, but I could hardly speak. Eli kept shouting into the phone (you had to shout when you called India in those days), "She's done it! She's done it!"

## THE WORLD

There were other trips to India. I visited Papaji several times in Lucknow as the students and disciples around him grew in number. Each time was unique as he continued to both confirm and challenge what I had recognized. He asked me to go door-to-door and speak to people and for the past twenty years I have done that. Without the grace of his presence and the clarity of his sword of inquiry, I would be still wandering in the heaven and hell realms searching for happiness while I avoided the essential longing of my heart. He is my guru, the true revealer of light. I owe the bounty revealed by the discovery of true fulfillment all to him.

Since my time with Papaji the world has been my home. I have visited and lived in many wonderful places. Whether in Maui,

Bali, Thailand, India, Australia, New Zealand, Scotland, Ireland, England, Germany, Switzerland, Austria, Hungary, Spain, Japan, Mexico, many states in my homeland of the United States—and yes, Clarksdale, Mississippi, too—I am at home. The yearning that felt so murky and ugly when I first became conscious of it has revealed the bliss of simply being. When I stopped running from the yearning or trying to cover it or change it, I could meet it directly and discover what it truly is. The yearning was a yearning for resolution.

Meeting directly is direct inquiry. Direct inquiry reveals truth. Truth is here and has always been here. It initially may appear ugly or fearsome, but in its core the truth is luminous and solid. It is who I am. It is who you are.

Before I discovered, through Papaji's grace and guidance, the ease of simply being, of being nobody in particular, I had a privileged life lived on a ground of inner suffering. In this discovery of the ground of endless spaciousness and peace, I live an indescribable life. I have the privileges granted to all who live in a free society, and I have the extraordinary privilege of discovering myself in everyone I meet. I don't always initially like what I see or feel, but in meeting whatever that may be, I continually discover the radiant mystery of life pristinely living itself through all forms.

## NOW

There is a story here now, but it is not the one I once thought, or hoped, or feared it to be. There are emotions that appear in this story, some pleasant, some unpleasant. There are wanted and unwanted events that happen in this story. There are accolades and disparagements. There is tranquillity, and there is upset. There are victories and there are defeats, just like in every other story. I had hoped that someday there would be no defeats, or unhappiness, or discomfort and in that imagined realm of elevation, I expected to find eternal bliss. What I have discovered is that there is no need for such a hope. What is always here, regardless of what else is here, is more than enough for deep fulfillment. I had feared that I was doomed to suffer the neurotic existence of the never-satisfied. That fear was the companion to my hope. Without need of the hope, the fear could not hold.

Whatever emotions or events or states are here, at the core there is always spaciousness of being. Allowing all, meeting all. Spaciousness was unimaginable to me when I sought rescue or escape. When I stopped making war, there was peace. When I stopped, it was obvious that the misery that first haunted me back in Clarksdale, Mississippi, was always—in the core—the natural expression of myself chafing at the various definitions imposed on that self. With no need of defining myself, I am free.

# CHAPTER 3

# Hidden Treasure:
# A Teaching Story

While reading or hearing teaching stories, it is usually advised to see an aspect of yourself in each role. Much like in a dream, you are actually each character. Also like a dream, everything is both literal and symbolic.

An industrious, conscientious man lived with his wife and children in a small village. To ensure a good living for them with savings for the unknowable future, he often traveled to different states. He worked hard and his work paid well. He was able to squirrel away half of his salary, and after many years his savings were a small fortune.

Perhaps the only failing of this man was that he didn't fully trust his wife regarding money. Or perhaps he knew her failings about money only too well. For whatever reason, he kept his savings hidden in a secret place and never mentioned that he had more money than what he gave her to run their comfortable household.

The family was happy. The children were being educated in the best schools in the area, and they showed promise for the likelihood of becoming responsible and happy adults. While they had the normal ups and downs of married life, the husband and wife loved each other and they loved their children. Harmony prevailed.

Then disaster struck. While on one of his frequent business trips, the husband was killed in a freak accident. In the very populous and often chaotic country in which this family lived, it was not unusual for hordes of people to be gathered together in unsafe conditions. On this unlucky day, the husband had found himself quite innocently swept up into a mob of religious zealots. The zealots became unruly, the police overreacted, and the resulting riot killed many people. In a horrible instant, the kind and loving husband who had always provided for his family was killed.

To make matters worse, he was killed with no identification on him. What he thought would be a simple evening stroll ended with his disappearance from this story.

After some weeks, the family became very worried. The weeks became months and then years. Everything changed. Since the wife had no knowledge that her husband had hidden treasure, she had no financial backup. Her family and her husband's family helped as much as they could, but after a few years without the husband's income the family was destitute. The children had to be removed from their schools and began to do the kind of simple, low-paying jobs that children can do. The mother first took in washing, but soon found that too strenuous for her health, and was reduced to begging from her neighbors just enough to keep the family alive. With this reversal of fortune their life had become miserable, and the future looked even bleaker.

The children resented the mother for not being stronger and more able to provide for them. They sorely missed their life of privilege. The mother resented her husband for leaving her in such a position—not even knowing for sure where he was or if he was still alive—and she resented her children for their complaining and bickering. Life was hell.

Unbeknownst to this unhappy family, a former business associate of the husband was busily trying to find where the family lived. He had grown worried when his very punctual business friend had missed several of their standing appointments. He feared that his friend had fallen quite severely ill, since when he had been ill in the past he had always contacted and canceled any appointments he would have to miss.

In was not an easy task in this vast and teeming country, but after some years and many inquiries he discovered the name of the village. He made haste to go to his friend. When he arrived at his old associate's home he was shocked to find that the husband had been missing for so long. He and the wife commiserated with each other, as they both realized that the worst must have happened.

After some tears and then some tea, the business friend looked around and was dismayed to discover such a state of poverty. The wife and children were in tatters. Moreover, they seemed sick and there was hardly anything to eat in the house.

"How can this be?" he asked the wife. "Your kind husband often told me of the money he had put aside in case of some unforeseen event. It couldn't possibly be spent. It was quite a fortune!"

The wife looked at him with cynicism. She wondered if he was cruel or just stupid. She knew without a doubt that if there were any fortune stored away she would know about it. What could he know that she didn't know! She knew that every cupboard was bare. She began to feel deeply angry at the presumption of this stranger and asked him to leave.

Dumbfounded, he left. But he returned the next morning and repeated his assertion that a fortune had been secretly put away for them. Again in humiliation and anger, fueled by her certainty, she threw him out.

But he persisted, for the husband had often proudly told him of how he was providing for his loved ones, and he knew the husband was trustworthy.

The children watched as their mother, in her certainty of tragedy, made war with the stranger's tale of redemption and bounty. The drama played day after day. Finally, the smallest child, a sickly little girl, asked, "If he's so sure it's here, why not get him to find the treasure?"

It seemed a good way for them to end the painful harassment of their family, because when he wouldn't be able to show the fortune, the stranger would have to leave.

# Hidden Treasure: A Teaching Story

To the entire family's surprise the stranger agreed. Although he didn't know where the fortune was hidden, he did know it was there somewhere, and he was willing to be responsible for finding it. And within a few days he *did* find it! Simply by lifting a few planks in the worn kitchen floor, the bounty of a lifetime was discovered. Another shock for the family!

The stranger didn't even stay the night; he slipped away as the family members were embracing with laughter and tears of joy. They would not have to beg! They would not have to split up and move to the city! They could eat and get medicine! The children could be educated, the roof repaired! They had the possibility of a happy future once again.

And when they turned to thank their benefactor—for they thought of him this way, even though he knew that he had only pointed out what was there all along—they found him gone. They were sorry not to be able to express their gratitude to him, but their overriding joy soon displaced this minor regret.

# Part Two

# CHAPTER 4

# Inquiry: Discovering Your Inner Nakedness

To define something is to know it, to encase it in meaning, and to gain some control over the experience of it. In the book of Genesis, Adam names the animals to know them as separate from himself. To know them as separate gives Adam power. To inquire into something is to open to it, to meet it, and to discover its meaning—or lack of meaning—from the *inside* of it. In many ways defining something and inquiring into something are at opposite poles of experiencing that thing. While radically different, they do complement each other. When definitions arise from the direct experience afforded through inquiry, the definition is a pointer to what is alive. When a definition is only mental, the thing defined is restricted to conceptual knowledge. A purely mental definition may be accurate as description, yet it lacks wonder and mystery.

It is impractical and unnecessary to inquire into everything to discover meaning. Definitions are the useful gifts of all who have gone before us. But when we turn toward truly knowing an emotion that we may have defined for decades, we can no longer rely on what we have been told. We must inquire *inside* that emotion to directly know for ourselves. Emotions, feelings of all kind, and the sense of "I" or "me" must be known from the inside to discover what *is* inside.

Inquiry as a spiritual practice is probably best known in the West as the recommendation of the Indian sage Ramana Maharshi, who was the teacher of my teacher, H. W. L. Poonja. Ramana used the term *inquiry* in a fresh and inclusive way to *stop* the activity of mind rather than to inquire *within* the mind.

I first saw Ramana's photograph at the Shambhala bookstore in Berkeley, in the late 1970s. I noticed his softly penetrating gaze and glanced at one of the books about him. Even with only a glance at his teachings, I recognized them to be the truth. But I couldn't imagine how what he was so simply offering could fit with my so complicated life. It seemed a teaching or practice for hermits or monks. I also briefly felt some fear that if I did dare go all the way with his suggestion, I might end up as an unmotivated renunciate.

At that time I was sharing in raising my eleven-year-old daughter and was afraid that I might become so content I wouldn't be able to fulfill any of my duties. I was also afraid I would lose motivation to pursue the thrilling event that had appeared in my life as Eli. We were intensely engaged in the early phase of our relationship, and I didn't want to miss the promise of deepening passion and commitment.

In truth, I was able to glibly dismiss Ramana's offering out of my own fear-based misunderstanding. It would take me another dozen years and meeting my teacher before I had the courage to investigate his invitation of inquiry. My fears were based in ignorance. I was actually afraid of my own fulfillment. By following the dictates of my fear, I succumbed to postponing true, lasting happiness. May all learn from my mistakes!

*Who Am I?*—the book I fled—is a beautiful transcription of Ramana's initial teachings, filled with the wisdom of an enlightened saint. Many have followed his counsel and used the question "Who am I?" to direct their attention back to the experience of "I." When directly experienced, "I" is discovered to be spacious and full rather than limited to the name that clothes it in a particular body and mind. The experience is astounding and liberating. Yet inquiry is more than one question, as profound and truth-revealing as that one question may be.

Inquiry is generally recognized to mean investigating, and that definition serves the purpose of this book well. However, it is not information that our use of inquiry provides, but direct experience. Inquiry that is only mental remains dry and formal. We need the energy and curiosity of a detective for full inquiry, but the result of this full investigation is known through our *experience*, rather than through subsequent definition.

Direct experience may or may not be followed by information as the term *inquiry* is generally used. Direct experience is unmediated by any information, and yet contributes to all information that follows it. Direct experience penetrates, regardless of whatever information may be placed in its way. For instance, we may have fearful thoughts about inquiring into the depths of our mind. After all, we could find anything! But when direct experience is valued more than thoughts, those fearful thoughts cannot bar us from inquiry. To directly experience anything we first have to leave behind all preconceptions of that thing.

No matter how often we are told *about* a thing, it is only when we experience that thing directly that we truly know it. We know the meaning of heat and pain and fire from the direct experience of coming into contact with fire. We can be taught that it is good to love and holy to show compassion, but those concepts will never have true meaning until they are real—our direct experience. We know a true kiss or surrender to an embrace when we directly experience them. We may practice or imitate kissing and embracing for some time, just as we may practice or imitate love and compassion before we have the direct experience.

In imitation or mimicry we remember what we should do or feel, and then we think ourselves through the act. "Now I press my lips, now I put my arms around . . ." In directly experiencing there is no thought. While thought processing is extremely important in many acts of a day—giving or following directions, remembering the time of a meeting, checking a grocery list, studying complicated issues, as well as the thousands of other sophisticated ways we think—consciously surrendering to any act or any moment requires the suspension of all thought.

## Inquiry: Discovering Your Inner Nakedness

We surrender thought spontaneously in moments of awe or shock. Usually our most prized memories are the moments when we are directly in an experience. Ironically, while our memories may be imbued with the flavor of the event, our memories can never give us the direct experience freshly. The image of the memory can evoke the emotional and physical sensations of the event, but when we add thoughts and concepts to that memory it is not the same event.

We can spend much of our lives in both pleasant and unpleasant remembered events, changing and rearranging them to milk them for particular physical and emotional sensations. Whatever bliss or distress we generate from memory, it is not the actual event. Finally we come to a time in our lives when we want to live our life fully present, rather than through our memories. At such a time, as sweet or self-defining as memories are, they are not enough. To directly live in the present, memories and the concepts that grew out of them must be suspended.

Moments of extreme focus and moments of complete open-mindedness are both without thought. In truth, thoughts stop many times within a day, but since our conditioned reference points are located in our thoughts, we generally overlook these moments of pure spaciousness of mind. We "think" ourselves from thought to thought.

To consciously choose to be without thought is the gateway to direct experience. If we are bound to our thinking process for our reference points of reality, we will ask only those questions guaranteed to keep attention on analysis, cause and effect, and conceptual evaluation. While recognizing the value and power of thinking, we can also recognize the power of actually choosing thought-free, direct experience. With this recognition, we can consciously choose when to direct attention to thinking and when to allow our attention to fall into thought-free open mind, especially in those emotionally charged situations that we have previously defined as choiceless.

People often fear being without thought as if it were the corollary to ignorance. Understandably, ignorance is feared. There is never a need to deny the harm that ignorance can cause, and use of the term *thoughtless* usually refers to some action taken without thoughtful consideration. What is overlooked in this corollary is the harm caused by being bound to thoughts. When we are bound to thoughts, our minds are already possessed by what we have been taught, by our latest conclusions, by beliefs of all kinds, and by our fear of having no thoughts.

The invitation to inquire into what is present requires that we have no preconception of what that is. Since we have spent most of our lives being taught to accumulate concepts categorizing what we perceive, this invitation is also a challenge. We are ready for this challenge when we recognize that conceptual thinking is limited. We are ready when we want more, and when we realize we aren't finding more in what we already know. This readiness, coupled with the willingness to explore, allows us to face the fear that naturally arises when we no longer rely on knowledge. If we don't rely on the knowledge we have for our experience of the world and ourselves, what is left? When we don't rely on our naming and defining particular emotions or particular states of mind, what is here?

As an intelligent species, we are directly familiar with motivation through curiosity. It is innate to us. Our inborn curiosity allows our infant brain to grow into its awaiting capacity. The more that innate curiosity is nourished by society and inner freedom, the more it naturally matures. When it is squelched by society or family, we become more lifeless and subject to being controlled by others' agendas. If learning is valued more than success, we flourish as human beings. When success with its rewards is valued more than learning, we learn to fear failing, and in that fear we wither at least a bit.

Too often our natural, animal tendencies to explore and discover get channeled into playing it safe or covering our inevitable mistakes. Sadly, to one degree or another this is the case for most conventionally reared and educated people alive today. We have been raised and educated to be tools and protectors of the interests of society. The interests of society are important! They are ultimately our own interests, as we are social animals. But the true interests of society are served when we have the space and permission to exercise intelligent curiosity.

———

While extraordinary scientists like Einstein report that their breakthroughs often come when they let all "knowledge" go, as in sleep or simply daydreaming, and artists of all mediums speak of creativity as a force that arises as a muse or divinity and then mysteriously directs the word or hand or body, our inner life usually remains off-limits to real discovery. The Buddha left his wife and family to discover what was missing in his life. Breaking this essential familial and social taboo and living a life dedicated to the discovery of truth led to his enlightenment. Rather than using his profound insights as an invitation to their own direct discovery, many followers of the Buddha only conform to particular beliefs passed on from his insights. This is usually true with all belief systems that begin with fresh discovery.

The Buddha and Christ, as well as all other cornerstones of religions, discovered and explored unknown territory, and their discoveries point to that possibility for us all. But usually their revelations are claimed as the final revelation, the opposite of supporting each of us to discover the unknown for ourselves. We cling to great beings' discoveries and revelations because they give us a deep sense of safety and belonging. We are saved from the horror of our own internal nakedness, and so we clothe ourselves in their sublimity. Our saviors do the work for us, and the result is too often inner laziness. We recite catechisms and mantras and memorize the insights of the saints of our religions. We may have relative peace and comfort, but as a result we may also deny ourselves the adventure of direct discovery.

Within every religion or school of thought there are courageous souls who have accepted the pull into the unknown and returned to overflow with the good news. Certain Zen masters and mystics of all faiths demonstrate the possibility for us all. Saint John of the Cross is one of many inspiring examples. In describing his own direct inquiry, Saint John sends from the sixteenth century a timeless message on the result of suspension of all believing for direct discovery: "I entered into unknowing. And there I remained unknowing. Transcending all knowledge."

This is not to suggest that inquiry should replace anything. Spiritual rituals and celebrations are nourishment for us personally and socially. Prayer soothes the spirit and mysteriously feeds our inner depths. Contemplative prayer is very close to silent inquiry.

Belief has its primary place in the developing person. When we have faith in what we have been taught to believe, we have the time and space to develop in other ways. However, at some point many people find that simply believing what has been taught—or substituting new beliefs for old—is insufficient. It is for these people that inquiry has attraction. Inquiry can easily be a companion to prayer, ritual, and celebration, and because inquiry doesn't exclude prayer and ceremony, prayer and ceremony needn't exclude inquiry. All are legitimate spiritual endeavors.

There is often a point in a lifetime, regardless of chronological age, when healthy, true doubt appears. We doubt what we have been taught, and we doubt what others insist we must believe. This healthy doubt flies in the face of the safety and comfort of fundamentalist certainty.

**Too often** there is little support for the deep examination that this spiritually healthy doubt demands. In my Episcopal confirmation classes—taken with other rowdy twelve-year-olds— the questions that we could ask with approval had little interest for us. The ones we were interested in—What exactly is the devil? Where is hell?—were considered disruptive and impertinent. Although the point of the classes was to bring us into the church in a more mature phase, for most of us it was the beginning of the end of our churchgoing days. Something essential in us was denied. I have heard countless variations of this story from others who felt their right to sincerely question had no place in their religion.

We have sometimes found that we have to rebel against *all* we have known, since those who "know" are unwilling to allow inquiry to be an essential part of spiritual development. In our rebellions, we absorb new anti-beliefs, and when we dare to doubt them too, we again are branded as heretics. How many converted Buddhists scoff at the naive Christians who believe literal interpretations of the Bible, while they themselves easily take on the belief of reincarnation? How many fundamentalist Christians brand New Age visualization as the work of the devil and revile Hindus with their nirvana and multiple faces of God, while having personal conversations with their deity and continuing their own visualizations of their version of God? Even proponents of inquiry often state what inquiry should reveal. In the "religion" of self-inquiry, the concept of nonduality takes the place of direct discovery. Authentic spiritual inquiry reveals the joy of fresh insights and revelation, just as artistic or scientific inquiry does, but if we cling to the latest insight as a *thing* we know, that thing grows stale.


Just as it is our human nature to think, it is also part of our nature to believe. There is nothing wrong with beliefs unless they serve to isolate us in the arrogant certainty that our particular beliefs are the one reality. And they usually do isolate us in both great and small ways. When we cling to old beliefs or switch to new ones while being certain that what we believe is reality, we keep our minds bound and we limit our life experience. When we are ready for deep inquiry, we have to be willing to at least temporarily suspend all beliefs.

To be of real spiritual value, inquiry must be alive and fresh. Regardless of what we remember or have discovered from the past, each time we truly inquire, we return to not knowing what the outcome will or should be. No doctrine is needed for discovery. No concepts of multiplicity, duality, or nonduality are needed. In fact, we must put aside all of our doctrines and concepts for our inquiry. All that is needed is the willingness to be unattached to the outcome, conscious, and truthful.

Deep inquiry is not for the fainthearted or weak-minded. It is for those who are ready and willing, regardless of fears and discomforts. It is the challenge and invitation to mature. It is the invitation to give up past reliance on others' discoveries while allowing those discoveries to encourage and even push us into our own inquiry.

Inquiry is not a coping mechanism. It is not present in human consciousness to provide certainty or comfort, except the sublime certainty that one has the capacity to discover truth for oneself. It is a stretching mechanism. It calls on the mind to stretch beyond its known frontiers, and in this way inquiry is support for the maturation and evolution of the soul. It frees us from the need to define ourselves to experience being ourselves. It is both humbling and a source of profound joy, but it does not provide a neat package of new definitions and stories.

The challenge in inquiry is to be willing to directly discover what exists with no reference points. Inquiry is no small challenge, for it requires facing the death of the inner and outer worlds as they have been constructed with no knowledge of what will take their place. We have the experience of releasing our constructed world when we fall into sleep, and we cherish and need this experience for our well-being on all levels. The challenge appears in releasing the constructed world while remaining conscious.

# Inquiry: Discovering Your Inner Nakedness

We all have been socialized to believe that what we are taught is real. Our view of the world and our role in it is the story that we begin to learn at our mother's breast. We take into our cells the story that supports the survival of our group, and we live in varying degrees of comfort and discomfort in our agreed-upon reality.

Those who have dared to cross the borders may be perceived as a threat to the whole, but they also serve to let us know the thrill of exploration. Throughout time it has been heretical to discover directly and then speak of that discovery. Yet there have always been those willing to be misunderstood, imprisoned, and worse, and blessedly they continue to speak.

The ones who leave consensual reality punch a hole in the fabric of what has been considered real. They sail off the edge of the known world, and those who return to us bring us reports of the permeability of the boundaries of knowledge. We may demonize them or we may worship them, but whatever we do with them, they show us the inherent fluidity of our knowledge.

In order for the rest of us to sacrifice our lives for our fragile and defended group identity, cultural and religious beliefs are enforced with fears of hell in the afterlife or fears of the present-life hell of social ostracism. Our fear of displeasing others, of being mocked, or even being killed is an electrified internal social corral. Social corrals are effective in keeping us safely in the realm of the known.

Since we are social animals, we replicate our social conditioning inside ourselves. Our internalization of social control causes inner torment and self-hatred. We define ourselves as sinners, or worthless, or unenlightened; conversely we are children of God, superior, and enlightened. Some definitions generate misery and some bliss, but all definitions are limited. We want to believe what we have believed for comfort and safety, or we want to cling to our new beliefs for what they promise, but somehow at a certain point in our lives we find our beliefs empty and constricting.

While the inner torment that usually accompanies outgrowing old beliefs and definitions may be quite uncomfortable, it is also a signal of the readiness for true inquiry. Earlier stages of simple, comforting belief are not bad or wrong, just as cocoons are not bad. Cocoons provide the particular necessary medium for growth and development. Yet if we refuse to budge when we have outgrown our cocoons, they strangle our freedom to doubt, to question, and to discover. If we can recognize our readiness and the discomfort that often accompanies it, we can support others and ourselves in being willing to let go of all belief structures so that we can inquire for ourselves. We can be willing to not know so that we can directly know.

Not knowing is quite different from either blind ignorance or cynicism. Pure "not knowing" is open and free, with abundant energy for inquiry. Pure not knowing is the mind naked of its concepts. There is no particular outcome in mind, as the mind is available for discovery. Not knowing as preparation for discovery is the antithesis of stupidity. Consciously not knowing, openly and freely not knowing, is the basis for intelligent inquiry.

As well as serving to keep us safe within our human herd mentality, our inner corrals subject us to inner staleness, and we become seekers of fulfillment outside ourselves. We seek material wealth, relationships, or respect even from a society or world we no longer fully respect. We seek knowledge and power. We seek phenomenal experience after phenomenal experience. We seek enlightenment as something that will give us more and more experiences. All of this seeking is an avoidance of the pain of our stunted inner growth.

We may be able to actually attain material wealth, relationships, and respect, but in themselves they are never enough. There is delight with each acquisition, yet delight fades when its cause is any object. We seek more, and often the seeking becomes even desperate. We accumulate some desired amount of wealth or fame or relationships or respect, and soon we must have still more. An addiction to more is the spiritual disease of our time.

Like all addictions, the beast of *more* is attempting to cover pain. Our dulled natural inquisitiveness is experienced as an emptiness we can only fill with what we know. We ask questions like "How do I get more?" or "How can I attract success to me?" We either glide or lurch to successful or failed attempts to have *always more*. Whether we are successes or failures we remain *essentially* unfulfilled, as we have lost the ability to directly, nakedly meet our own emptiness.

Our teachers and leaders may preach to us about our inner

needs and even point to the futility of trying to find lasting satisfaction in acquiring more. However, usually what is offered are more and different objects of knowledge and belief. Rarely are we supported in direct discovery. Rarely are we directed to questions that require an open mind.

**An open mind** requires losing rather than gaining! If our concern is gain of more, whether material objects or objects of knowledge, experience, power, or even enlightenment, we continue to rely on the goal of *more* for our fulfillment. The open mind empties itself of all knowledge of what will provide satisfaction. When we are willing to let go of all ideas and dogmas, we have a chance to inquire.

In this way inquiry requires meeting death. The death of all we think we are and think we know is required to discover directly our deepest experience of who we are. Natural intelligence dictates that the fear of death is instinctual in all organisms. This fear directs us away from whatever may lead to nonexistence, and it serves us well. Most of us want to live at any price. Even when we are suffering and feel that death would be a refuge, most of us instinctually move toward life and away from death. Without discounting the validity of this core fear, we can still recognize when thoughts generated from the fear of death keep us from living life freely.

To truly inquire we must be willing to die for an instant, to release all preconceived notions and opinions of what we need, of what is true, of who we are. At that moment we directly experience that which exists yet needs no definition, no belief, and no defense for its existence.

When fear is perceived and—if even only for an instant—you stop relying on your conceptual knowledge of fear, what is the experience? If experience of a body with its sensations is perceived and—for a moment—you don't name that body or even know "body," what is experienced? When we ask these questions of ourselves and follow our attention underneath the knowledge that has categorized all particulars, we are *inquiring*. When we inquire, the inner and outer terrains of life experience open in inconceivable ways. Life is lived not without thought, but without thought controlling life experience. Fresh, original insight follows direct experience. The thinking process is enlivened by the spaciousness available to think freely. What has never been thought can be thought. Inner space and outer space are no longer artificially separated by thought.

When we are willing to inquire directly into fear, which is to some degree or other always a fear of death, we have choice. Willingness to stop thinking about fear and to directly experience fear is the gateway to freedom. When we remain unwilling to directly face fear, we are at the mercy of the thoughts generated by that unwillingness. ("I could really die, I could lose everything, I shouldn't tempt fate, I'll do this later, this is too much for me. . . .") With the freedom to choose, we can choose to continue to obey all fear-based thoughts, we can repress those thoughts and expend our life force denying fear, or we can take a moment and inquire directly into fear. With the freedom to choose we can tell the truth about our choices.

Fear generates thoughts that serve to define our life experience by safety of some kind—physical, mental, or emotional. And yet there is no final safety in life, so fear and its attendant thoughts work overtime. Inquiring *into* fear while casting aside the attendant thoughts opens the experiential gate of freedom.

To inquire into fear—or any emotion—requires that we go into it with full, undistracted attention. We have to stop whatever we are thinking *about* fear—where it comes from and why, what it means, how to get rid of it—and directly experience the sensations we have labeled "fear." Without the name "fear," there is a force field of energetic vibrations waiting to be experienced. This force field is composed of the same substance as the discoverer of the force field. Whether you inquire directly into fear, or the *I* thought, or any other emotion or phenomenon, conscious life discovers itself!

We really can put aside all that we have been taught about who we are and inquire *into* ourselves. We can cherish our inner curiosity and trust our intelligence. We can be willing to make mistakes and even be utterly wrong as we open our minds. We can use the same rigor and forthrightness in our inner lives as any artist or scientist uses in professional pursuits. We can dare to open, to suspend belief, and to stay conscious as we discover the substance of every emotion and every phenomenon revealed under the microscope of our inquiry.

When we have discovered our capacity to open and fully inquire into anything and everything, we can inquire into the supposed boundaries that appear to separate everything. What is the true substance of separation? It looks real, it feels real, and the consensual reality is that we are separate from one another, from nature, from God, from enlightenment, from everything. But when you inquire into the boundary of separation itself, what is discovered? When we don't allow our sensory information to be the last word, isn't there more to be discovered?

When we don't rely on any belief—regardless of how closely the belief comes to an interpretation of reality that comforts or confirms us—we can be open to discover what is at the root of all experience. We can tell our stories with the willingness to undress them. We can dare to discover pure unadorned nakedness. We can discover what changes and what remains the same. We can finally ask, "Who am I?"

The teaching story "Hidden Treasure," your story, and my story can all be read and heard in the context of discovery. Where does each point? What does each expose? Where is each coming from? They all converge in the silent open core of you.

## CHAPTER 5

# Harmony

The very word *harmony* evokes equilibrium, peace, and the natural coming together of various forces. The result is an uninterrupted flow of life energy for the nourishment of body and soul. When we idealize harmony we imagine the dynamic and yet smooth melding of opposites. The music of life supporting us, internally and externally. The balm of a tropical breeze. Floating in the peaceful, friendly ocean of life.

We do seem to have some echo within our memory of the hum of the universe soothing us. We can imagine the embryo in harmonic fluid with the swoosh of the mother's blood and the rhythm of the mother's heartbeat keeping time to the growing self. There are waves in this sea. The heartbeat changes with the mother's different physical and emotional states, the neuropeptides vary according to the mother's emotions, and accidents happen that are sometimes fatal. But if we consider this period of incubation generally, we see it as a time and place of harmonic support for the uncountable changes in the growth from embryo to fetus to baby.

Deconstructed, harmony shows itself to be composed of both stress and relaxation in balanced relationship. Parts that on their own may be jarring can together form a harmonious whole. All of nature is a great mix of differences, and when the mix is harmonious, it soothes and relaxes us. Winter is often harsh, but without spring it would be bitterly unbearable. Individuals may be adrift and stressed on their own but harmonious in a couple, family, or community; individual aspects of a person may be disconcerting but experienced as part of the whole contribute to the depth and lovability of that same person.

When experience is primarily harmonious, we have the sense of being held, either internally through our own equilibrium, or externally through the alignment of supportive outside forces. With too much rest, we lose the stimulation necessary for development. With too much stress, we lose the rest necessary for development. In harmony we have both. In harmony there is innocence, regardless of a person's actual age. Things seem to follow a pattern, and we are securely central to that pattern.

We read and respond to the possibility of the dynamic equilibrium of yin and yang, the three gunas, and the principles of light and dark. We reminisce fondly about times when we felt in harmony with all around us. We yearn for a unity that is echoed deep in our sense memory. We search for protection without confinement, connection without limitation, knowledge freed of learning. We romanticize nature as a place of pure harmony and spend time in nature drinking in the nectar of the so-called natural world. Floating without drifting, endlessness without ennui, and activity without inertia all reveal the harmony of senses, perception, and emotions. We gravitate back to our version of the womb.

The harmony of a period in our lives is often only recognized in retrospect, after disruption appears. Quite often the harmony we experience is exclusive to us or to our group. To maintain our sense of harmony we may have to ignore the suffering of others. In service to the fear of losing our own harmony we know how to practice denial of what others suffer. The 1950s in the United States are usually referred to as a period of harmony. Compared with the massive disruptions of the Great Depression in the 1930s and World War II in the 1940s, it was harmonious. And yet at that same time there was great suffering and injustice for many groups of Americans. Relative harmony depends on conditions, either conditions prior to the relative state of harmony or insulation from surrounding disruptive conditions. Relative harmony, by its nature of being relative, or conditional, does not last indefinitely.

If we contemplate harmony without succumbing to our idealizations, we can recognize that the harmony we remember, the harmony we objectify in memory, is relative. The family in our teaching story lived a life of relative harmony until disaster struck. In our teaching story the family's worldview is limited to simply knowing they are provided for. Or, in the case of the

father, that he is providing. This limited view is bound to be challenged, and in our story it is. For our purpose, this view represents the relatively innocent and unseasoned soul. Our teaching
story family lives in an insulated version of heaven, a harmonic
realm accompanied by the sense that this is how life simply is.

Idealizations are problematic as they point to what is whole
and complete in itself without allowing for the disruptions that
both frame and contribute to that wholeness. Neither "nature"
nor our lives are as neat as our idealizations. The sweet harmony
we love alternates with the discordant and sometimes chaotic
movement of our lives. True wholeness includes all rather than
excluding the messy, unwanted parts.

In my earliest memories, Mammy—my maternal grand-
mother—was the essence of harmony to me. When she was near,
all was well. Whatever discomforts of life may also have been
present, she was the reconciling force. Her smells, her big, moist
eyes (her eyes!), the deliciously soft folds of her untoned body,
and her words of love and support made a haven of harmony for
me. She and Granddaddy would come to stay with us in Clarksdale for weeks and sometimes months; they lived with us at the
end of their lives until it was unbearable for Mama and Mammy
to be together. As a child when I got word that they were coming,
I would sit by the dining room window all day if necessary, waiting for the first glimpse of their car.

It's not that conflicts never appeared when Mammy was

around. Life and all the chaos of our home life continued, but her presence provided a safe space in the midst of conflicts. She *was* the space I could effortlessly be myself in. Without needing to search for love or support, I was able to grow. It was a kind of outside womb experience. With her, my identity, though unformed and immature, was composed of particles of love. Throughout her life she remained a source of love for me—one that I all too often took for granted. She was a beacon of pure light in some dark times. I was very lucky. With her, being me was just fine. Mammy served as a kind of marsupial pouch for me. I would go on my way when I had enough nourishment, but could always return for safety if needed.

We need these external wombs if we are to grow into healthy adults. And we find them in many different ways. Safety and nourishment are found in diverse situations: in friendly social contact, cuddling, warm baths, daydreaming, and playacting. We later reestablish them in sports, close friendships, marriage, and perhaps a secret, inner life. They are what both religious and secular communities are commonly based on.

Pleasure is certainly an aspect of harmony, but pleasure can accompany many states. Harmony is found anywhere we feel safe and cared for. In such a place neither safety nor care is even considered.

We may experience the harmony of being "lost" in things as diverse as a project or a sunset. I love the experience of being lost in a great book or a movie or a performance. Music of all types can strike the chord that provides harmony. When we are swallowed by the beauty or power of a work of art of any kind, our usual preoccupations with safety and comfort are gone and we experience relative harmony. Safety and comfort aren't the issues. There is no issue; there is just the freedom to be, and the freedom to grow and learn. The freedom to be touched by the vast— and even chaotic!—mystery of it all. (Of course there are great works of art in all mediums that evoke the opposite of safety and comfort. They serve a different though equally essential function.) States of harmony that are evoked by a particular alignment of conditions come and go, just as the experience of the freedom that accompanies them comes and goes.

At many times in my life I have felt the bliss of harmony through bodily sensations. Dancing, swimming, and making love produced times when all was felt to be deeply and truly well. I have felt it with physical exertion and with physical rest. And I have relished those feelings. Relished them so much that much of my life became oriented around recovering them.

When I discovered meditation, I discovered that being still— while still awake—also sometimes produced a state of harmony. Likewise, when I smoked marijuana and briefly experienced psychotropic substances, my identity, with all its fears and concerns, would temporarily disappear. The problem was that when I stopped meditating, or when the induced trip ended, the harmony was replaced by the chaos of my thinking mind. Then I would seek work, or dance, or nature, or lovemaking to bring back the harmony that came and then went so easily.

But what happened if I couldn't find meaningful work, if I couldn't dance, if I was injured or ill, if I was stuck inside a city with no access to what I called nature, and what if lovemaking no longer was as magical as before? Well, then I suffered and sought new and different ways to provide the harmony in which my concerns of safety and comfort stopped causing me to suffer.

The search for losing myself, of feeling safe and free, distracted me from the inner and outer discomforts in my life. I wanted harmony more than I wanted deepening or learning. I either avoided or waged warfare with any irritant that kept me from my states of pleasurable harmony.

It was useless energy expended, of course, as harmony is only part of life. My very search for harmony would become irritatingly disharmonious. The search for peace, or happiness, or even love can itself become the chaos the search is initiated to avoid. Finally I had to face full-on the discomfort that led me to deeper experiences of life.

This habitual pattern of seeking pleasure and then finally giving in to pain began when I was very young and continued in varying degrees until I met my teacher. Even now, I would certainly rather experience pleasure than pain, and I am almost certain most other creatures of all species would too. But when pain appears I now know better than to unnecessarily avoid it or make war with it.

As we accumulate knowledge, power, and other means of survival, we construct our defined identities. For all of us, these identities, composed of infinite and complex images coupled with sense impressions and emotional imprints, grow into the central sense of "me." My teacher, Papaji, and his teacher, Ramana Maharshi, called this central identity the "I" thought. We all have it.

When we say "I want," or "I did," or "I am," we are referring to a collection of definitions accumulated over time that represents who a human person thinks he or she is. It may be starkly individualistic, as in the case of most of us from Western societies, or it may include others, as in the case of many tribal and religious cultures. Whether exclusive of others or inclusive of particular others, it is the thought or collection of thoughts defining who one is. It is a safe landing area, a place where we can regroup, where we can feel that we are seen. Allowing for outbreaks of upheaval, it is in general a place of harmony, a place of rest—at least for a while. Without it in at least some degree, there is no sanity.

This collection of "me's" whether experienced as the complexity of "myself" or as the discrete members of a family—however strictly or loosely defined—provides security through recognition by those connected to "me." This social cocoon does provide nourishment for growth. When we feel connected to a group, we feel protected. Even a group where there is little knowledge of the particulars of the individual, such as many church groups, study groups, political groups, advocacy groups, etc., offers the sense of belonging. Even the collection of people only seen irregularly in a neighborhood or town, whose names and histories remain unknown, can be a social resting place. At different times in my life I have felt the solace of leaving an argument or an internal state of distress just to walk to town and both see and feel other people. We see people in cafés and sitting on stoops or in front of huts all over the world, and we recognize the harmony present. We take internal and external provision from our groups, and if they are supportive of the potential of individual and collective discoveries, they are even more nourishing.

In your past there has been at least enough harmony in your life that you survived, you learned to read, you learned to take care of yourself. Even if you found your harmony only in deep sleep, you are lucky that that amount of harmony has been in your life. Whatever harshness may have been part of your life, at this point your environment, including this book, is supporting your growth and development. At this very moment you are in a safe enough space to read and to contemplate what you read. There is enough harmony supporting you that you have the freedom to meet, to directly experience, both harmony and disharmony, pleasure and pain. You have the time and the inclination to consider deep questions. Relative to many, perhaps most people in the world, you are living a life of harmony.

The characters in our story were enjoying their harmonious life, but they are not portrayed as being self-reflective enough to recognize what they had when they had it. When I was little, I didn't recognize that not everyone had a source of love as bright as Mammy. I didn't recognize how precious she was. She died when I was in my mid-twenties. I did know what I had lost then, and was racked with regret that I hadn't done more to make her last years more comfortable. Perhaps our teaching story characters really recognized the bounty they had only with the shock of losing it, but by then it appeared to be all gone.

Losing Mammy and regretting my insufficient care of her while she was alive was the opposite of harmony. And it taught me my first lesson of the capacity we have to tenaciously overlook what we have until we lose it.

However secure and loved I felt with Mammy, I didn't want to stay by her side most of the time. For maturation we need more than harmony. There are disruptions to relative harmony that are essential for our inner and outer growth. The disruptions may be invisible to anyone else, or may be present for the entire world to witness. They may be as small as an unwanted noise that distracts you from your reading, or as abysmal as the suffering that accompanies tragedy. Whatever their apparent size, disruptions are—in their irritating way—necessary reference points for the harmony that precedes or follows them. Often the most disharmonious disruptions to harmony herald the possibility for a more meaningful, presently unperceivable, life.

Using our teaching story as metaphysical model, we see that in initial harmony inner life is still in infancy. It has not been tested by life other than the stress that is in interplay with rest in harmony. This is a larval stage of development. The time of feeling safe, protected by what we have been given and have accumulated, is usually a time of scarcely any self-reflection.

Self-reflection, along with humbling, usually comes only when harmony has been disrupted.

At some point in many lives, however hard or easy those lives have been, the harmony we have known is disrupted by an inner call to open to something unknown. When we hear and heed this call, whatever degree of harmony we have in our lives is not enough to fulfill us. We are actually called to disrupt our relative harmony for the sake of the unknown. This overthrow can be quite terrifying and can appear reckless to those around us and even at times to us. If it is a true call for inner growth, it *is* disruptive to the boat of defined, protected identity.

It doesn't appear that any of the characters in our teaching story have had such a call, but then the call isn't necessarily visible from the outside. It can be active without anyone else knowing. We suddenly—or finally—can't live the life we *should* live, marry the person we *should* marry, think the thoughts we *should* think.

Within the harmony of our teaching story family, perhaps the mother yearned for a different life at times, one more like the one she had imagined as a young girl. Or perhaps she did feel quite lucky with the staunchness of her husband and her healthy family around her. While our story doesn't support a particular viewpoint for her, we can imagine any number of feelings she may have had, because she is standing in for each one of us.

While her life may not be appealing to us in its particulars, we can each imagine ourselves living a similarly harmonious life. In her culture, she lived a life of plenty. She was provided for. She did not want for food. Her children were being educated. She was not in apparent danger for her life. War was not being waged around her. No one in her family was suffering from torturous disease.

Is this true for you, now? Is there relative harmony internally? Externally? There is no "correct" answer. These questions are here only to support your assessment of your internal and external worlds, but you are invited to reflect on the harmony around and inside you that allowed, or is allowing, you to develop as you have.

If you make the skillful assumption that your external life is at present harmonious enough, you can more accurately examine your level of satisfaction with both your inner and external life. If you are in complete fulfillment with your whole life, can you remember a time when the external aspects were in harmony and some discontent was surfacing from deep inside you?

**And when** we look closely at the provider of this relative harmony for our family? The husband is clearly diligent in his duty, but what of his relationship with his family? We know that he doesn't tell his wife of the hidden treasure; does this point to deeper rifts between the two of them? If he cannot share the reality of material bounty, is there also much else he keeps hidden? Let us put ourselves in his place, with our life story as his, and see. We are free to imagine ourselves in his role, with our habits of sharing and hiding.

We don't know the husband's inner life, but we do know that as well as withholding crucial information from his wife, he traveled frequently for his work. The surest condition to breed discontent with some aspect of our lives is the discovery of other lives being lived more freely. Perhaps he had heard of a Buddha, or a hero, or an adventurer. Perhaps he had met someone who had tasted unconditional love, or someone who lived a life entirely out of his realm of experience. It is part of our nature as humans to wonder and to imagine our life freed of its relative constraints. When we meet someone who has—or even only appears to have—a promise of liveliness unknown to us, we are liable to catch a spark of it. That spark can spell destruction or disruption to our harmonious, protective cocoon.

While it is possible that the husband merely traveled for his work, was happy that he could return home, and felt lucky that he wasn't attracted to any other life, it may be more to the purpose of our inquiry to imagine ourselves as the husband waiting for some idealized future when all duties have been completed. When his wife was fully provided for and his children well married, then perhaps he could examine what he truly wanted for his life.

We do have duties and responsibilities in our lives as husbands and wives and parents and children. We have duties as citizens and community members. We have duties to the world at large and to all the unborn children yet to come. Without diminishing the importance of these duties, we can also discover if there is an even greater duty to open to an inner call.

And what of the children in our story? What of your life as a child? Whatever the dysfunctions of your particular family, you did survive childhood. Many don't. Whatever the hurdles and challenges, whatever the real traumas, you survived relatively intact.

We know even less about the children in our story than we know about the mother and father. We know they were fed and well educated, and felt entitled to the harmony their parents provided. We know that when disaster struck, they childishly and peevishly complained. As they were children, they behaved as children. They had led relatively pampered lives. They had been given what they needed before they knew they needed it.

To enter their lives, we don't need to be literal children. We can recognize how we too have behaved as children when what we assumed was innately ours has been taken away. A disruption in harmony can lead to sobering and humbling reality. How quickly we assume entitlement to the blessings of food, education, and relative freedom. How much more quickly we assume we should be able to have what we want, since we have always had it. How essential to discover the fallacy in that egoistic equation.

For mature growth it is essential to discover that the world isn't partial to our desires and needs simply because it has seemed to be in the past. An obvious, hard fact. Through tantrums and magical thinking, even including the more childish aspects of religious belief, we normally try to reclaim what was taken from us.

In our story the children never show us if their disaster contributed to a deeper understanding. But you *as* the son or the daughter can discover in yourself, from your own disasters and from imagining yourself as one or both of these children, if you have gained some wisdom from losing what was precious. Or you can discover if you are still at war with the fact of losing what was felt to be *yours*.

**Harmony is essential** to replenishment of body and spirit. When we enter the harmony of deep sleep, our personal life is absorbed into the spaciousness of no-mind. When we are replenished, we naturally awaken to the forms of life. Because we have tasted the peace of being absent while sleeping, we know the fulfillment of rest. When our conscious life reasserts itself, we can meet it all the more fully from our time of not having had a conscious life!

In our waking life we know the bliss of sensual dissolution in the ocean of physical and emotional love, as well as the bliss of floating in the rhythms of actual oceans and lakes and rivers. We know the harmony of bodily and emotional well-being. We know at least moments in a day, or a life, that are spacious and free.

Through the cycles of harmony, disruption, and return to harmony, we recognize that in harmony there is natural, free happiness. When we are conscious of harmony, there also usually appears a desire for more. When we lose harmony the search for it begins. As we are creatures endowed with the great power of thought, we begin to try to think our way back to the happiness of harmony. We search for particular circumstances that will give us pleasure, and we do initially experience harmony when our desires are met, but only *initially*.

Since the harmony that is experienced through the acquisition of a pleasure object is relative, it is invariably followed by its own ending. We search for more or different pleasure objects. More sophisticated objects; objects of knowledge and unique experience, expanding our knowledge of what can and cannot give us more and more pleasure. We hope to find a pleasure that will not die. We search for absolute harmony and we come up empty-handed.

**When we recognize** that relative harmony always has a beginning, middle, and end, we can appreciate that the disruption to our relative states of harmony, however much unwanted, is merely part of the whole. With enough maturity of experience we can stop expecting the cycle of *harmony/disruption/return* to be different from what it is. Disruption, or reversal of fortune, no longer needs to be fought, and can even be welcomed as the natural order of things. Our attention need not be stolen by thoughts of what was, why it should have lasted, or what we can do to bring it back. Attention is freed to fully discover what is always here, whatever degree of harmony or disharmony may also be present.

Absolute harmony is unconditioned by events that come and go. There is no disruption and no return. The absolute underlies all conditions and stories because it is the substratum. It is space itself. It is only in our identification with sensations, feelings, and emotions that are connected to our ideas of who we are and what is happening to us that absolute harmony is overlooked. Of course the *only* used here is huge. This *only* is held together by the fabric of individuation, one of the greatest and most powerful phases of conscious life. Individuality is a marvel in itself and is also limited by itself. It is a phase that has an end. It ends either in physical death or in the realization of oneself as one with the substratum of all phases.

The chaos of birth begins a lifelong story of chaos/equilibrium/harmony/disruption, a profoundly familiar rhythm of life that we know and revisit on both physiological and emotional levels with almost every stage of growth and development of our lives. As soothing and essential as harmony is, depth demands disruption. Harmony is disrupted for life-forms to grow out of their larval stage.

Whatever our early lives were like, hard or easy, they were shelter for the emerging sense of self. As you grew in age, your awareness of yourself as "somebody" grew. Maybe you had the great good luck to be sheltered in love and tenderness, and your sense of yourself developed easily and naturally.

Many of us have less than ideal sheltering, and that too has its own kind of horrific grace. When shelters are bleak, or at least less than fully nourishing, the edge of uneasiness that accompanies our growing sense of self leaves the sense that there is a hole where there should be wholeness. We may feel a diffuse sense of vulnerability. We attempt to fill the hole inside us with any number of temporary plugs. We learn to be more lovable, or to know more, or to be tougher, or to need less, or to pretend that all is fine.

The holes in our cocoons prove to us that something is needed, something is missing. We attract or are attracted to others who represent the missing fibers of a web of safety that left in us an indelible imprint of absence. We hope these others will give us back what we lack. And in harmonious phases, we do feel whole again, but the lack within us keeps insisting that nothing and no one can permanently fill it.

When we are willing to stop avoiding the pain of this absence, when we are willing to stop making war against this absence, when we are willing to stop dramatizing it and stop filling it with pleasurable objects, the absence turns out to be the direct way to experience the living presence of wholeness. The hole we experience can call us deeper into ourselves in pure inquiry. It can reveal the insubstantiality of the perceived "me" needing protection and completion. The hole itself, when experienced directly, is the window into revealed self-knowledge.

So whether our formative initial nine months and then first years—our cocooning—were beneficial or harmful, we mostly lived in harmony relative to the disruption that followed. At the end of our first cocooning, after our time in whatever kind of womb we inhabited, the placenta burst. The onslaught of the hormonal sea at puberty ended whatever kind of childhood we lived in, the realities of adulthood disrupted our idealizations nourished in adolescence, the aging or disease of the body ends the sense of physical self as indestructible. And when we look back with the perspective of the present, we can see that each stage had its layers of protection that the following phase destroyed.

Do we learn? Mostly we haven't, although wisdom has asserted itself in bits and pieces along the way. Mostly we have fought every disruption and longed for what was lost. Mostly we have been surprised and even offended when disruption has appeared. Can we learn? Certainly, and it is time. Disruptions can actually be met fully. Rather than longing for what has passed, we can assess what we have lost and be open to what is next, bearing whatever pain any transition may bring.

This is not a recommendation for simplemindedness or New Age naiveté. Global disruptions demand attention of the highest order, and many of our personal disruptions do too. There is the possibility of all that is good being lost in any disruption, from the ending of our time in the womb to the ending of an era. Disruptions are often infinitely complex, occurring on many levels, while the relative harmony that came before appears simple in comparison. The point is to realize that in cycles of growth and development all harmony that is subject to disappearance is temporary. Disruption and harmony are part of the same whole.

When we no longer simply mourn the phases that have disappeared or fight the phases that have appeared, we have the maturity to discover what is not lost in disruption. In this discovery, a deeper, inner harmony is revealed. It isn't augmented in relative harmony, as it isn't lost in disruption of relative harmony. It is absolute.

**The immaturity** of the family in our teaching story is a reflection of our own immaturity. Teaching stories mirror us back to ourselves, if we allow them to. We can see how the family lives in a bubble of prosperity, little suspecting that anything could disrupt it. When there is disruption, we see how immaturely, although normally, they all deal with it. We see how that immaturity deepens the suffering of the loss.

It is unlikely, and unnecessary, that any of us will tell ourselves of the transient nature of harmony when it appears. It is natural and recommended to fully rest in harmony, to be fully nourished by it, and not to look toward a future when it will be absent. Disruption of the harmony is signal enough to realize that relative harmony just doesn't last. Disruption is the dharma bell that calls our attention to surrender. For if we surrender to the disruption as we did to the harmony, our pain of loss will not grow into suffering. If we recognize what is involved in trying to cling to what has already passed, we can simply stop the clinging.

These points of inquiry are here for you to explore how periods of harmony appear, and disappear, quite naturally in your life. The questions can support you in being conscious of harmony while it is present, as well as being conscious of the deeper harmony of your life that allows you to meet disharmony in a way that supports inner growth.

1. Are you ever aware of the state just before awakening after a restful sleep? Where do you experience that pre-awake state?
2. Do you recall a period, either in the present time period or some time in the past, when you were just mindlessly "rolling along" without noticing those around you except as minor characters in your story?
3. Are there particular feelings associated with that time?
4. If so, can you experience those feelings directly, without any narrative about them? Where are the feelings located in your body? Without judging or rejecting, allow your attention to penetrate any feeling you are presently aware of simply as energy or vibration. What is revealed?

# CHAPTER 6

# Reversal of Fortune

The most substantial growth, as well as the seeds for self-destruction, occur in the shocks of life. Shocks most often deal with unwanted changes of circumstance and subsequent loss. Even when shock follows an apparent gain (winning the lottery), the result is the loss of familiar ground, or identity. When shocks are plainly negative in nature, they usually lead to identification of oneself as a victim and an overwhelming sense of injustice, but shocks can also serve to catapult us into inner growth.

Anger and cynicism may take hold and become the worldview, as in our teaching story and in my story, or surrender and humbling of a prior sense of entitlement may begin. Humbling of the mind is essential for spiritual insight. With more insight comes the possibility of more fully and freely participating in the world, without the weight of self-inflation. With insight it is natural to become more clear-eyed to the realities of life.

**There are** horrendous reversals of fortune that are occurring daily all over our globe. There are the horrors of genocide, massive and individual victimization, and destruction of innocent lives and fortune through natural catastrophe. There is the full spectrum of suffering caused by the tyranny of particular governments, revolutions, ideologies, or economic systems. As individuals we may feel helpless in the tide of both local and global destruction. And in many ways we are helpless.

Our own suffering may seem puny when compared with the suffering of so many others. When we rightfully mourn just the horrors of our own time—the Holocaust, the torture and murder of the Darfuri, the Congolese, the Cambodians, the Rwandans, the Bosnians, the Kurds, all other persecuted groups and countless individuals—we may decide our own pain is trivial. By even addressing our relatively puny suffering, we may feel ourselves to be selfish, and conclude that our suffering is not quite legitimate. Certain religions and social movements teach us to pay no attention to our own suffering. We are taught to just help the others who need so much, or to just be concerned with our community's well-being. But the burden of our own individual suffering, whatever its comparable size, actually keeps us from being able to clearly and fully help others.

When we suffer, whether "legitimately" or "illegitimately," our energy and attention are bound up to some degree in that suffering. To be willing to tell the truth about our own suffering, and to be willing to face that suffering, frees energy and attention. Before that freeing, all of our activities are informed to some degree by the distraction that comes from denying or indulging our suffering. We work for peace while we are at war within, and therefore our peace work is tinged with war. We give help when we need help, and the help we give comes with our own needs. The invitation here is to step back from the comparisons of whose pain is bigger or more "real," and simply inquire into our own experience. In this book the teaching story and my story form the planks of the platform that can support that inquiry.

The birth of my baby sister shocked me out of my mindless, harmonious existence. Before she was born I had the secure and attention-getting role of baby girl. My older brother, the crown prince of the family name and lineage, was the star, but as baby girl I felt both his protection and my parents' love. That seemingly permanent security was suddenly reversed when my sister was born. I was six years old and was clearly aware that my mother was pregnant and that soon there would be a new baby in the house. But when she showed up, I realized the new, sweet, adorable baby was not good news for me. For the first time I became conscious that circumstances could threaten my well-being. I didn't know what I feared, but I did know I was no longer in a friendly world. There was another creature who had replaced me as the center of the universe, and I didn't like that at all. The household suddenly revolved around the baby's needs, and rightly or wrongly I felt excluded from the circle of love. I was furious. My sudden temper outbursts only got me punished and more excluded. Then I began a perpetual pout. Not a good strategy for winning affection.

I was always a skinny kid, but in the months after the birth of my baby sister I began to get even more so. I had no appetite. No matter how much berating came from Mama and Daddy and even Mammy and our maid Susie, who was a source of comfort in my early torment, I simply could not drink my milk. It was revolting to me. Finally I was threatened with being sent to the Preventorium. The Preventorium was an institution situated next door to the TB sanatorium in Magee, Mississippi. While it had originally been designed to help prevent TB in sickly children, by the time I was sent there it was also used more generally. In my parents' case, the specter of polio was more relevant than the fear of TB. This was the late 1940s, before the polio vaccine had been discovered, and fear of polio haunted both parents and children. My twelve-year-old beautiful cousin went from being a boisterous tomboy to being confined to an iron lung when she came down with a particularly virulent strain. The Preventorium was a place where susceptible children could be nourished with good food, fresh air, and exercise into a vigorous state of health. So it was said. We children knew it as a threat of misery, much like the threat of going to hell if we were bad.

I couldn't drink my milk or clean my plate, though I did try.

My parents followed through on their threats and sent me to the Preventorium. And it was hell. We lived in dormitories, sleeping in iron beds with high railings. It seemed to me that none of us wanted to be there, although some quickly adapted. I didn't adapt. I still couldn't drink my milk, and I had to wear horrible bloomer-type shorts. Even though I was only six years old, I was already embarrassed to hear that in the summer we would have to go topless. I prayed to be released before summer. It was a horrible time for me and seemed endless, though I must have stayed there only three months or so. I felt totally abandoned, had no friends, and the food was even more inedible than that at home. I cried every night. I said my prayer to Jesus: *Now I lay me down to sleep. . . .* He was my last hope of rescue.

**In our teaching story** we observe one family's particular reaction to a reversal of fortune. Reversals of fortune can come slowly over time or suddenly. Our story has a sudden reversal, but the reactions to that reversal appear in the fabric of life that has been woven over time. With retrospection we can see that all reversals have threads that extend back into time and yet show up suddenly. As we know from our story, there would have been no reversal of material fortune had the father simply included the mother in his plan for future provision. This one thread in this family's life caused the other, more apparently harmonious threads to begin to tangle.

In this chapter and the one that follows, the entire family can be viewed as a diorama of personal reactions to negative change. As in all stories that influence you, you are invited to enter the characters so that the story is about you. Again you are invited to put yourself in each person's shoes to see how they fit. All of the characters in all stories can accommodate each of us. Finally we find ourselves in everyone.

After all, each person in our simple story must have complexities beyond measure. Each has at least points of light or brilliance, and each has his or her moments of darkness. Each has desires, frustrations, victories, and defeats. When we are willing to recognize how alike we are in emotional and mental structure, the form that structure assumes is not so foreign. We may not speak the same verbal language, but we all have drives, and instincts, and emotions. Our cultures may be radically different, but we are all human creatures. As human creatures we want both connection and protection. When these are in alignment there is relaxation and harmony; when they are in conflict, choice arises. When tension from lack of either connection or protection is present, potential for everything from continual escalation of conflict—insanity or war—to immense inner growth is available.

No one wants negative change, but since it does appear in life, it is extremely useful to recognize both the normal feelings and the surprising potentialities it evokes. For while we may feel helpless and distraught in our reversals, we have millions of years of evolutionary adaptation in our cellular knowledge. We may not know what to do in any particular moment, but an essential ingredient of our innate intelligence is the capacity to freshly discover.

In our story, protection is lost, and negative stress appears. We see that the family reacts in the usual ways. They add additional suffering to the pain of their reversal. As we witness the tragedy of their continuing to meet negativity with more negativity, with our perspective as reader and observer we can discover another choice. Fresh choice requires willingness to experience the pain of loss, and in that experience to discover what is untouched by any loss of fortune. This may not be the instinctual choice and it is not the normal choice. Yet it is available to each of us.

The characters in our story are oblivious of this choice, and as a young child I had probably never even heard the word. I wasn't given choices; I was told what was going to happen if I didn't drink my milk. And it did happen. Since I really couldn't drink my milk, the concept of choice was foreign. By entering into different characters' oblivion or powerlessness, we can discover how we remain ignorant and helpless in our own stories. May their and my oblivion serve to awaken us all to our deeper capacity to bear the truth of reality, and in the bearing, to discover the conscious and unconscious choices we make regarding our experience of reality. May the possibility of these choices pull our attention to the very substance of reality. In that discovery may we more fully realize the truth in the core of us all.

When we read of the wife/mother in the story and we put ourselves in her role, we don't need to suspend our own personalities or habitual reactions. The story is told simply enough that there is ample room for you—as you know yourself—to find yourself in her. You can still have your personality with your particular likes and dislikes and talents and dysfunctions while also being this wife/mother.

Can you imagine yourself as this woman prior to the reversal? Without knowing any particulars of how exactly you are provided for, you are provided for and quite comfortably. Just as we don't need to understand the properties of oxygen, or even know that it exists, to be nourished by it, we don't necessarily know the properties or even the existence of what provides for us in other realms. As an essential comfort that had continued for some years with only minor changes now and then, none of which were explained to her, there would most certainly be a sense of security, whether conscious or not.

Even if you are an overly anxious type, in our story your anxieties have to do with less important issues than your basic provisions or even your essential need for air. In your own story, are your anxieties about having enough oxygen or water, or are your anxieties relatively more superficial, while seeming essential? If so, you can know this wife/mother as yourself. Being her, you recognize that sometimes you or your husband or the children are ill, sometimes your household is not as well kept as you like, and sometimes your husband or children irritate you. Sometimes you may even dream of a more exciting life. But whatever natural pains and pleasures appear at times, the security of more than enough food, shelter, and opportunities for your family is the ever-present background. You have the leisure and the good fortune to be concerned more with details of life. And then it all changes.

In our story it takes some time for the reality of change to sink in. Our wife/mother has been provided for long enough that when it doesn't happen as usual, she doesn't register that fact fully. We all have the capacity to initially deny the occurrence of loss. Her mind gets busy with explanations of delay; she worries about possibilities of her husband's illness. How would you react? What would you say to yourself? How have you reacted when your world has suddenly, through no fault of yours, turned upside down?

With no intimation, no reason, no explanation, your world collapses. The provider does not return from wherever he goes to gather the provisions. (As if the air you breathe no longer fulfills the needs of your physical being.) It is at this moment in the story that you discover what your first reaction is to this enormous change.

**At some point** in a negative reversal, we become aware of the panic behind the worry. How long it takes before the sense of loss and vulnerability sets in may vary from person to person, but at some point it is recognized that the source of prior security is not present. If actual love is also part of your version of this wife and her partner, then this sudden, unexplained absence adds the additional emotional ache of loneliness and a possible story of abandonment.

All of these reactions are normal. There is nothing wrong with them. A wife who relies on her partner, and is perhaps deeply connected to him or her, will naturally worry and miss him when he is unexplainably absent. Since humans are social, interdependent animals, the pain of loss is natural and can be observed in all social animals. There is no need to assume that this pain wouldn't or shouldn't be present. We are attached to each other in infinite ways. When these attachments are sundered, we experience pain. The natural pain that accompanies severe loss is not what causes our suffering. It is what we do with that natural pain that gives rise to unnecessary suffering.

**In my story** I felt I had been banished while the rest of my family was together in happiness. The fact that I had been unhappy before my banishment did not appease the suffering. Even though unhappy, I had felt protected. Now for the first time I felt vulnerably alone. I was terrified and angry and sad. I had good reason to be. And that was all I knew. I didn't have the resources of a mature mind to discover how to make the best of this bleak situation, though some of the other children did. The advice to meet the pain of my loss more deeply than I was feeling it would have terrified me even more. My nervous system was already overloaded, and I did not perceive any alternative. I was a child, and I needed the comfort children need in times of loss. Or did I? Perhaps it is more skillful to realize that this horrid time was the setup for the grace that followed.

Whatever the retrospective evaluation, at the time it was miserable at the Preventorium and I responded miserably. I suspect it would have been an unpleasant experience regardless of how I framed it in my mind. But I made it even worse than it was by the conclusions I drew and by my allegiance to those conclusions. There is no blame intended in recognizing how I contributed to my suffering. I didn't know what I was doing. I didn't know better. Now I do.

Let us examine being each of the other members of the family in our teaching story. Perhaps the children don't notice the absence of the father at first. From the skeleton of our story we know that he was often absent for his work. We don't know what kind of father he was when present, so here your imagination can substitute your own father. Even if your father only provided you with the sperm necessary for your birth and then left, you can experience being provided that and—unless another father entered your life—then being abandoned.

Whether your father was in the background or the foreground as a presence of love and support, whether he was a cold and unforgiving taskmaster, whether he was a good or an insufficient provider of life support, the provider of some sort of security is missing. At the same time, you realize that your mother is tense and worried, and you find her crying at odd hours. What happens when that which gives us life support is no longer here as it was before? When you, in your identification with the children in our story, finally recognize that the source of essential safety is missing, what do you feel?

For those who relied on their father as a source of love and recognition, for those who loved their father and felt his love, his absence and the mother's distress are traumatic disturbances. Just as those who are connected with aspects of the natural world mourn the loss of an essential element, we mourn what sustains us. The hole left in the heart is undeniable to those who know unquestioned love and then sense the disaster of its absence. If you can't conjure such a love for a real or fictional father, can you imagine the sun disappearing? You have experienced cloudy days before, but this time is different. With each passing day there is a deeper sinking in your chest as it becomes more evident that the sun is not behind the clouds; it is gone.

If the mother and the children relied upon the father for the sustenance of life and find themselves becoming unmoored, each in their own way—you in your own way as you enter the story—what of the father? You can be the father as he faces his last moments in life. He was young once, with good or bad or indifferent parents. He had some sort of experience of childhood, and adolescence, and maturity. We know he married, but what of his life, inner and outer, before that marriage? From what we know, he lived a responsible life, doing his duty, providing for both the present and the future. Was he a secret poet, a philosopher, a genius? Did he love to dance? To take early morning walks? We know in the last hours and minutes of his life he was the victim of a religious mob, but was he drawn to the gathering because of some deep spiritual need or was it an unlucky coincidence? So many details of a life that we can never know.

At what point in his tragedy is he willing to recognize that his future is finished? Maybe he has only an instant, but as our story is meant to be flexible enough to include our participation, we can allow it to be an instant that stretches long and wide. His last moment can include the essentials of his life. What has his life been about? Has he regrets? Is there anything needed to be passed on that has been held back? We know he should have passed on the information about his provision for the future, but what of his inner self? What can he tell us in his last moments of his essential being? What has really been important in and to his life? What last words would he hurl through space to his family, to his parents, to his world, to his gods?

We may not be able to say what he would have wanted to say, but we can put ourselves in his place and know what we want to say. We know for sure that he didn't have the time to do the things he may have wished he had done or say the things that may have needed saying. Knowing of his lack of time is our gift for whatever time we have left.

With you in the father's role, and in the moment of the realization of certain death, what do you send those you leave behind?

In this instant, in even the small death of the past instant, what remains to be said? Why not take this moment, put the book aside, lie down, and invite the experience of being at the end of your particular life story. Whatever is appearing before you, whatever regrets or satisfactions are passing before your eyes, where are you? What is your substance?

**The Buddha's** timeless statement "Life is suffering" would have no meaning if change were not the essential ingredient of the stuff of life. Our stuff is not limited to material things, including our bodies, but also includes our relationships, our feelings, our ideas, and every other aspect of our world. To cure the disease of suffering, the Buddha's prescription was non-attachment. And there are those who are not attached to their world and do not suffer. Does this then condemn those of us who are attached to our world to a life of suffering? No. Directly inquiring into the core of suffering is another, equally potent medicine.

Taking the medicine of nonattachment requires rigorous dis-cipline. Likewise the medicine of inquiry requires a particular rigor. It is the rigor of the willingness to discover the truth of something—the "I" thought, any feeling, sensation, emotion, or *other*—without relying on any definition for its discovery. We can know we hurt with pain, and if we are willing to not define the hurt or the pain or even ourselves, we can discover the nature— the substance—of that hurt, that pain, that "I." Suffering that comes with reversals can be fully met, and when suffering is consciously and fully met, it is no longer suffering.

As disruptive and unwanted as change can be, change and loss are often the essential catalysts for awakening. Reversals can shock us open. Suddenly we are forced to see beyond our prior view of life. Even the longing for fulfillment, peace, or enlightenment occurs because our earlier complacency has been disrupted. We can no longer childishly expect the world to conform to us. For a fully lived life this expanded view is essential.

Theoretically this is easily understood. The challenge, with the profoundly valuable resulting benefits, is to be willing to directly experience unwanted change full on. To dive into the belly of the beast of loss is a more direct and vital experience than merely accepting loss. The more direct the experience, the less is thought about the experience. In open, conscious, thought-free experience, it is natural to discover what lies at the core of all loss and all gain. A willingness to open to what is unknown, though it may be perceived to be annihilating, is required. This is facing death. Facing death down.

When we are willing to meet change on its terms instead of our own, we can feel the pain of loss and not be condemned to *suffer* with this pain. Suffering requires a personal narrative with heroes and villains. It requires a resistance to reality *as it is* through the thinking process. By referring to memory or fantasy, both of which are stories, we "know" what reality should be.

When unwanted change appears in our lives, we—as adults—have a choice. While both the change and the probable pain that comes with it may be choiceless, choice is found in our relationship to pain. Counterintuitively, if we open our minds in surrender to pain (surrender is not theatrical indulgence) we discover it to be ephemeral. The suffering of loss dissipates and reveals the substratum of spacious, open mind.

It is the very shock of change, with either loss or gain, that is its greatest gift. In the period before we experience how quickly everything can change, there is usually a sleepy entitlement regarding life. Like the family in our teaching story, we meander through our lives, enjoying what bounty there is with no real recognition of how precious and brief everything finally is.

As human inhabitants of the twenty-first century, we are bombarded with messages of what we don't have. We may succumb to those messages, especially if we see that others have more. Television and advertising of all kinds play on and feed off this tendency. But if suddenly we had not enough to eat and no time to rest long enough to read a book, we would recognize our present privilege for the blessing it truly is. It is the nature of humans to take for granted what we have, to feel it is our due, and subsequently, if it is suddenly lost, to feel pain in the face of such radical change. That normal reaction can be the springboard into the root of suffering, and from that root into the ground of being.

———

**Change is** the most incontrovertible fact of our world, yet it is the fact we most go to war with and suffer from. We may yearn for it, or fear it, or be devastated by it, but rarely do we meet it as the fact that it is. All that moves changes. All that is born changes. All that is thought, or felt, or experienced, changes. All events, all views, all struggles, all plans, *all things* change.

Although we may never have to face losing everything, we can recognize how even losing *anything* has the capacity to generate pain and suffering. We lose replaceable yet loved objects and we mourn; we lose our place in line and we fume. Our candidate loses the election and we decry the theft. The list can go on and on. Rather than make facile value judgments on the superficiality of our complaining, we can actually meet the pain that is generated from the most superficial of losses as well as the greatest. In this way, our neurotic preoccupations as well as our truly great losses can serve to awaken us.

Reversal of fortune is inevitable for all of us in many ways. With the mystery of luck and grace, the reversals are manageable, and although we may mourn for what has been lost we are not devastated. We adapt to the change and open our minds to discover the nourishment and beauty that is still here. Perhaps there are other positive changes that give us gains, and our attention is temporarily freed from what we lost. Perhaps we truly realize that change is simply a part of life and we have the maturity not to unduly dwell on what we no longer have.

—————

All of us, of any age, know the experience of loss with either temporary or permanent change in well-being. Temporary or permanent disability and disease are great teachers of the ruthlessness of change. We usually fight the change, and either rejoice when our emotional or physical body returns to its former state or we somewhat adapt.

Some changes are not so easily incorporated into our life stream. With devastating changes we can feel as if we have lost the meaning of our life or that we can no longer find our inherent vital force. When you have lost a loved one, or lived through any of the many horrors of being the attacked or the attacker in any kind of war, or of being hated, or of being abused in any form, it can feel as if a major part of yourself has been ripped out. It can feel as if the pain has ripped open a hole in the fabric of your being and the life force has flown out of you. The drain of continuing to live can be experienced as further loss.

Regardless of the cause, the ache accompanying the loss that change brings can be all pervasive. However we may spend our time avoiding it or covering it with activity, the diffuse and particular pains too often remain in place to haunt us. However we may rationalize change and loss, the pain of the fact of loss can feel intractable. However many alternative universes we imagine where it didn't happen, until it is faced as it is, it continues to taunt us with its recurring power. In dreams and memories it announces its hold on us. As we revisit it or run from it, it remains in charge. We believe it to be the master of us.

It isn't. When met fully without either resistance to the loss or hope for return of what was lost, astoundingly and simply, the ache of loss is revealed to be insubstantial. To meet the loss nakedly, we have to reclaim attention given over to the story of loss. The story we tell about our loss—even if the narrative changes over time, even if the narrative includes the eventual benefits that occurred because of the loss—only serves to keep the feeling of loss intact.

Only when we are willing to open our minds and consciously enter into the pain itself do we discover its insubstantiality. There may be other feelings waiting underneath the initial pain or there may be the spaciousness of the open mind, but the particular pain attached to the story of loss cannot survive being directly met.

What ultimate good are words of comfort when you feel profoundly that you have lost something essential to your life? When you are a child, words of comfort can give temporary refuge, but when you are an adult, they are often hollow. Our meditation practice can give us periods of relief, but if our narrative of loss continues once we are away from our practice, we still suffer. Our friends and our philosophies can assist us with gaining the right perspective, but where are they when the demon comes to call at four a.m.?

Support groups and therapy can help us to see the patterns of suffering and help to unwind those patterns. But if and when we are truly helped in getting through one loss, unless we discover our capacity to open directly to pain, the next big change or loss will generate the same suffering. The next big loss will generate even worse suffering if we had assumed that once we were healed of a particular loss we were then immune to future loss. Or we find ourselves cautious, guarded, and wary in a useless attempt to stave off any future heartbreaks.

For it is heartbreak we are dealing with here. We certainly don't feel pain when we lose the things and situations we don't love. We invite the change and loss of ill health, negative emotions, and abusive circumstances. We seek positive change and suffer when it doesn't come soon enough.

In either seeking or avoiding change and mourning the loss it brings, we fight an endless, useless battle through the activity of our thoughts and behaviors. We become mentally and spiritually exhausted with the Sisyphean struggle to control life.

And life rolls over us.

We can metaphysically decide that all is perfect, or God makes no mistakes, or karma determines our fate. We can affirm that we will attract only good things by thinking that we will attract only good things. Or, as proposed in this book, we can meet what comes into our experience with no need of any system of belief. We can directly inquire into what is presently here without determining if what is being felt in this moment is good, bad, perfect, karmic, choiceless, or pure illusion. If we surrender the need to classify experience, even for a moment, we have the capacity to inquire *into* it. We can use our attentive energy to expand into the state or feeling we have been trying to control or avoid.

Understanding does follow, but it is understanding from the

inside out. When we are willing to not know what a particular feeling really is, we have the possibility to inquire into it. Curiosity of the unknown is natural to us when we don't follow thoughts of avoidance. Direct discovery generates both immediate insight and long-term understanding.

Our education, our habitual way of thinking, is to first know what something is and then decide what to do with it. Of course this is perfect and time-saving in countless situations. We don't have to reinvent the learned information of the generations that came before us. As an intelligent species we have made extraordinary advances and have accumulated vast knowledge in all fields of study. Science and technology have contributed to us through disciplined, strong thinking and learning. We have learned there are basic rights for humans and all living creatures. We have learned techniques for better communication, for better management, and for better citizenship. We have learned what it takes to be better teachers and better students. We have learned that tolerance fosters cooperation. We have learned what our destructive, consuming habits can do to our planet.

However, when the matter at hand is deep personal pain, all our learning ultimately fails us. It is direct experience, predicated on *conscious not knowing,* that opens the gateway to fresh discovery. After all, we do know that change is natural and inevitable for all life-forms, but when it comes to *our pain,* this abstract knowing is useless. Being thrilled by the changes that continue over millions of years, recognizing political movements that rise and fall throughout history, following the arc of a continent, a nation, or another person are little help when change emotionally hits home.

---

**In our story,** reversal of fortune does hit home. And the bad luck is seemingly irreversible. However the family as individuals and as a whole deny it, fight it, or wail about it, they are left without apparent provision. They have lost their innocence. And, as sweet as innocence is, temporarily losing it is essential for maturity. Mature innocence is not based on being unconscious and entitled. It is discovered after fully passing through the fire of loss.

**The questions** that follow are offered as support for directly meeting any residue of resistance to change and loss in your own life. They are best answered freely and unedited. There are no "correct" answers, and the answers don't even need to be factually true to be relevant. It is sometimes helpful to work with a partner, taking turns asking and answering each question many times.

POINTS OF INQUIRY:

1. What have you lost?
2. Are you aware of having gained anything from your loss?
3. Is past loss still directing your life story or self-definition in any way?
4. Is there any perceived danger in giving up your story of loss?

5. Are you willing to live without replaying in your memory the story of what was lost?

6. Where is the feeling of "loss" in your body?

7. If you meet this feeling of loss fully, letting go of the narrative of *what* was lost, what is experienced?

There may be layers of emotion waiting to be met. You can open fully and meet each feeling that appears. Be aware of the tendency to begin telling a story, either familiar or new, to avoid the direct meeting. Just release the story and let your attention penetrate the feeling.

# CHAPTER 7

# Hell

In the darkest waters, without a life raft, losing strength of inner purpose and yet recognizing that far from the end being near, this hell world is endless. No hope, no help, no understanding. Adrift yet without the dreaminess of drifting, senses are sharply acute, overstimulated by sounds, sensations, and thoughts with both body aches and body dullness. Heat to the point of burning or cold to the point of freezing. Dry as dust and dripping with the rot of lost dreams, there is no relief. There is an urgent need to escape yet that need is accompanied by the piercing recognition of no possible escape. Inner torture is perpetuated by memories of *what once was* accompanied by vainly searching for the prevention of *what is*.

Hell is not madness, although it is filled with elements of madness. It is not delusional, although there are inner torments that mimic delusions. There is a stark clarity in the descent, with both fear of madness and willingness for it to be madness, for with true madness there is the possibility of a treatment. A treatment means hope.

Hell is a hopeless desert of the soul, even while external functioning may keep hell's deeply personal suffering from the general view. A nightmare surely, but each day reveals that the nightmare is waking as well as sleeping. A depression, a psychotic episode, a spiritual emergency, a dark night of the soul, or simply reality? Whatever label is placed on this experience is limited and finally of no use.

How did we find ourselves here? Was there warning? If so what could we have done to avoid it? What in the universe generates such a space and why? How could any benevolence anywhere allow such inner suffering?

Where there were friends, there are now only adversaries. Where there was space there is now sticky confinement. Where there was certainty of a continuing future of possibility, there is now the prison of damnation to this dire, impoverished present.

Hell is the name throughout time that has best described this inner torment. Only this hell can humble the arrogant mind.

Like most people who reach adulthood, I have been through some hells in my life. The first I can recall was when I was six. I had been sick with a childhood fever and was napping in Mama and Daddy's bed. When I awoke, I could hear my new baby sister crying. The crying was terrifyingly loud. Even though she and my parents were downstairs and I was upstairs, the crying—screaming really—filled the room. I became very, very frightened and ran into the big closet to hide. I don't know how long I stayed hidden, but finally the terror passed and I had the nerve to go downstairs. The family was gathered around the kitchen table. There was no crying or screaming now, and they welcomed me into the gathering. I asked about the crying, but no one could recollect anything remarkable about the baby and her crying.

After that mysterious event, I began to have more terrifying experiences. Simple noises would get very loud and terrify me. Then I would feel my body disappearing. First it would go through a series of alternating sizes, from huge to hair-thin. As I felt it begin to disappear altogether, I would run for help. My mother was no help. She was as confused by my horror as I was, but we had a wonderful maid, Susie, who became my refuge. I would put my head between her ample breasts, she would hold me close, and I would feel safe again. My "fit" would pass.

However the experience is categorized—anxiety attack and out-of-body experience are the diagnoses I have at different times applied to it—it was pure hell for me at the time. We each have our versions of hell, and perhaps they are similar in their horror.

In our teaching story, the hell realm was evoked by losing a life of bounty. But hell realms are not limited to material deprivation. Hell claims its population from all strata. In the wealthiest and most powerful societies there are as many suffering from personal hells as in the poorest. Although having our basic needs met provides protection from the hell of poverty, there is no real protection from our inner hell realms.

**For our purpose** of deep inquiry and investigation, it is in the inner realms of hell that we discover the most essential truths. For fight our inner hell as we might, it is relentless with its internal lashings that are all the more brutalizing in their invisibility.

Hell is the most dangerous of inner realms because we can be tempted to give up our souls here just for the possibility of release. Or we can learn to dully survive in hell without receiving the ruthless teaching that hell has to offer. We can attempt bribing our notions of a god with promises of being a better person, we can swear to ourselves that we have learned our lessons, we can grovel before some inner Satan to try to get at least a better position on some rung of hell, but to truly receive the teaching of hell, we have to be still in the midst of its misery.

We have to stop squirming or screaming or sobbing or fighting long enough to consider what hell could have to offer besides more suffering. That question is our point of inquiry.

When there is some degree of willingness to look into the maw of hell rather than to follow the natural instinct to flee, there is the capacity to discover the deepest teachings. The deepest teachings, by their very nature of being the deepest, must be able to be found anywhere. Hell is where we don't want to have to look.

**Throughout history** we have received reports from those who have descended into the belly of this beast. Great artists of all mediums, great mystics certainly, and ordinary people like each of us have experienced at least the rim of hell. From Christ's bleeding suffering and wail of forsakenness to the paintings of Goya with their gruesome proof of the hell of war to the stark eyes of tortured prisoners as they "confess," we recognize that which we most fear. The painful suffering of anyone whose world has collapsed in the face of loss of any kind—as well as the mysterious onslaught of inner collapse with no external cause—finally proves to us that hell is a common and horrendous fact of life.

Since to live life truly and fully *all* of life must be met intimately, what is it that our hell has to teach us? What do we learn from empathizing with a crucifixion? What do we learn when recognizing the horrors we as a species and as individual humans are capable of from Goya's paintings? Often we don't learn. Perhaps a savior does appear and as good people we are released. Or maybe we find ourselves miraculously delivered into tranquil rest. But when we don't learn, we are haunted by the memories, however hidden they seem. And, more important, we can learn. We can open our minds even in hell. We can discover the truth of what remains changeless in the worst circumstances.

Psychological literature is filled with descriptions of the patholo-
gies of hell along with the current recommended treatments of
choice. But the psychological approach is usually one of discovering or assisting escape and relief. This approach is certainly
appropriate and recommended until you are ready and able to
actually learn what hell has to teach. For discovery in hell we
have the extraordinary good news of Christ's surrender and
ascension. We have the exquisite poetic expression of union with
the divine under the most grueling and degrading circumstances
from Saint John of the Cross. We have Ramana as a sixteen-year-
old boy willing to meet death. We have joyous testimony of those
who have "crossed to the other side" in every spiritual or religious
tradition. You have *yourself*, to the degree you are willing to be
taught by whatever hell you may find yourself in.

For some, hell is sustained over a period of years or even
decades. For many it lasts for weeks or months. For some it
appears, disappears for a while, and then reappears. Some are
haunted by the memory and possibility of its return. Some generate a quasi-hell as a kind of living amulet to keep the real hell
at a distance. Some sense its presence underneath the relative
peace of a prosperous and conflict-free life. Some have heard of
it through religion, and fear their damnation into it. Some have
scoffed at the notion of it until they have experienced it first-
hand. I have never met anyone who has not at least tasted hell.

The taste is enough to send one running—into numbness,

into feverish practice of rites and rituals, into inner nightly calculations of the likelihood of that day's actions sending one deeper into hell.

Hell usually makes its unavoidable presence known by appearing unannounced and unexpected. The periods of our lives that are uneventful or supportive can lull us into a self-absorption so narcotic that we don't imagine that destiny has anything other than good for us. In spite of religious teachings and subconscious tastes and nightmares, we really can't imagine the bitter medicine of hell until it appears.

How long can we bear it? If we are resisting it, our capacity is limited and we have to get help. Drugs, sleep, distraction, and support and love from friends and counselors all have their place in the natural need for distraction from this internal war with an immutable force. But if we aren't at war with hell? If we are actually—even for a millisecond—willing to be at peace in the midst of this tremendous misery, an immeasurable capacity is discovered. In this millisecond of surrender, quite different from resignation, light is discovered in darkness.

How many hells and mini-hells have we already been through? Perhaps the time spent being born, being thrust from the womb, is our first experience of hell. What infant hells are being experienced when hunger is not immediately satisfied? And the times when babies are miserable for no apparent reason? Maybe those early preverbal cries are our first bodily experiences of abandonment in need. Most of us have memories of periods in our lives that were experiences of internal hells. Perhaps some degree of hell has always accompanied birth and growth, or the next step. An aspect of the invitation of this book is to consider hell a natural part of our human experience. As such it can be directly met and investigated.

If hell is considered natural, though certainly unlikable—like a particularly severe winter or a miserably hot, crop-killing summer—we remove the stigma of *damned* from it. Without this superstitious judgment, we are much closer to finding the courage and capacity to open our minds to receive hell's teaching. Being aware of our learned superstitions is an important part of seeing how we fabricate our version of reality and are then bound by that fabrication. Our superstitions often work underneath our thought process, but fear of unexplained reality always supports our superstitious tendencies. If we are willing to open our minds when fear is felt, we no longer need the protection of our beliefs. When we are willing to cast aside our superstitions, we are willing to face reality directly.

When we take a larger perspective, we can see that there are periods of better times and periods of worse times, in both our inner and our outer worlds. And if some hell periods are certainly the result of foolish or mistaken behavior, there are just as many that arise with no known cause. Surprise attack. As in our teaching story, out of the blue.

In a true meeting, which is a true investigation and true inquiry, our prior *ideas* of the meaning of an experience have to be suspended. Our concepts and evaluations about the causes of a feeling or an emotion have to be put aside if we are to get to the *essence* of that feeling or emotion. We have to be open to really not know *why*. When we are willing to not know, we can more fully open our minds and with conscious intelligence inquire *into* and discover.

Most of our concepts and judgments of hell, or even of the minor negative emotions that assert themselves throughout the experience of life, have to do with proving that we are essentially bad, or doomed, or permanently flawed in some irrevocable way. We have been taught this by parents, school systems, religions from the East and the West, and by our own internal idealization of the purified being we hope we can be. This mass of conditioning is only in the way when real investigation is needed. And real investigation is needed when we are willing to hear what any deep experience, especially hell, has to teach.

How do we meet or investigate what is by its nature terrifying, unlovable, abysmal, and liable to swallow us into its muck? The "how" is actually simple. The real challenge is the motivation. Why would we even want hell's teaching when we can distract ourselves with so many options, or at least cover our heads and wait for it to pass?

We are ready to meet the worst (hell) in ourselves only when we are ready to be free. Before that readiness we will hide from the worst, or dramatize the worst with a tragic melancholy. Or we may deny it altogether. The thinking process of our brain is filled with powers that allow us to decorate reality or dodge and cover whatever may threaten our version of reality. These powers are to be admired and used creatively until we really want to live freely. Then we must recognize that what keeps us in inner bondage is our fear of what exists in the naked core. If we have been secretly frightened by our unknown inner beingness, and if we have been taught that our inner nature must be tamed into submission because of its potential for selfish evil, we will keep our conscious attention separate from and be afraid of the innermost core of ourselves.

Usually even if our upbringing has been more enlightened, and we are taught that we are essentially pure and good, the wild, untamed parts of our personality are likely to frighten us enough that we keep them hidden in shamed secrecy. They show themselves in nightmares and in hell.

To be willing to turn toward "them"—"them" being the aspects of ourselves that we separate from our outward self-image—is the mark of maturity, which is the readiness to be free. Not free of "them," but free of all inner and outer definitions of what "they" are. When we are free of our conceptual definitions of ourselves, we are free to be fully whole. We then directly know ourselves as undefined, *indefinable* consciousness, freely being itself. When we are willing and ready, hell is one of the most important teachers to point to that freedom.

---

In our teaching story, members of the family in hell turn on one another in frustration and blame. The radical notion to stop the blaming and complaining and to simply descend into the experience of hell in the spirit of open investigation doesn't occur to them. Instead they seek release in turning on one another, and in that turning, they sink deeper into the mire.

This is a familiar habit known to us all. When the unbearable appears in the world, rather than face the worst and explore it directly and freely, we attack what is nearest us. We vent our frustrations with the agony of the circumstances on others through blame and irritability. Our helplessness feels unendurable, and finding a scapegoat is the age-old strategy of momentarily feeling some sense of control.

The shallowness of our teaching story family shows us the futility of our own strategies to avoid our worst fears through aggressive displays of power. Until we are aware of this avoidance, we will continue to refuse responsibility for our circumstances. We will continue to find someone or something to blame. We will blame other people, the planets, our genes, God, and the devil. We will blame anything to release the pressure of hell. In the disbelief and horror of our circumstances, we prefer conspiracy theories to the openness of simply and directly discovering what the worst is made of.

When there are no outside others to blame, we internally fragment and attack ourselves. All of the blaming and attacking is a futile attempt to make sense of or control the horror of the suffering. Deflecting and blaming may take the pressure off for a moment or two, but in the process it sinks us deeper into the ignorance of hell.

Being able to respond is identical to being able to investigate. Both require openness and willingness to stop whatever story we are consciously or subconsciously weaving about *why* this horror has happened and who is to blame. Initially it certainly may be necessary to discover both why and who, because we intelligently want to know the causes of abysmal circumstances. But in direct investigation of what is in this moment and what it can reveal, the sole concern must be *what is*. This is when the clear response is the direct investigation. The focus is fully on the moment itself, regardless of the level of suffering or the causes of that suffering. The response is the question, "What *is* this I am experiencing as hell?"

Although the family never gets to this level of maturity, you can if you tell the truth to yourself. Do you want to be free? At some stages in our lives we don't even know or care what true freedom is. All we want is protection and attention. We want a safe cocoon where we can simply live and grow. There is nothing wrong with this. All creatures go through stages where without protection and attention they would not survive. Human children need an extensive protective stage before they are able to survive on their own. In the legitimate immature phase freedom does not serve. All creatures also naturally outgrow this stage as they are called to maturation. Many who have outgrown the protective stage still cling to the security of the cocoon. Sometimes young eagles even have to be forcibly pushed by their parents from the protective nest to learn to fly. There is surely at least an instant of hell between losing everything, falling, and then finally flying.

**At the dawning** of spiritual maturity, as in biological maturity, a push or even a shock is often necessary to provide the catalyst for essential growth. The birth of true knowing follows the death of the previously known. What was previously known may have been true in its time, but when finished becomes false knowing or ignorance.

It is not always so easy as to simply put away what we have outgrown. We don't often choose to leave a protected place. Although some things are easily put aside or easily fall away on their own, transformational leaps take us, or throw us, into unknown territory with no reference points. The baby eagle may or may not have noticed that his survival depended on his protectors flying back and forth with his nourishment. Flying may never have been considered in his baby bird brain. Likewise, we may have never noticed that throughout time, in all cultures there have been sublime examples and stories of living freely. Spiritual nourishment prepares us for flying, but we only fly when we take the leap, or are pushed, into the unknown.

We may feel an internal pull toward what is calling us in this unknown realm and be terrified of it at the same time. Or we may ignore the pull altogether until we find ourselves losing what we never considered could be lost—our nest—and desperately fighting the unknowability we are left with. The more we give our attention and life energy to fight the unknown, the more we experience hell.

When we can recognize that the soul matures naturally and sometimes with pain, we can be more willing to recognize the space between one phase and the next. Usually we desperately try to cling to what no longer is, or deny that we have lost everything we know, or attack those around us in anger and fear. We overlook the spaciousness in the shift between one reality of life and another. If the baby eagle doesn't resist falling then the moment of falling before flying is just as sweet as flight. If we don't resist whatever is being experienced, then the underlying sweetness of life is found even in the most bitter parts.

**We can't know** beforehand that even in the worst the best can be discovered. But we can discover the truth of that. We can try to remember our discovery for whenever the next change occurs, and that memory may be somewhat useful. But to directly know what is here in this moment, all memory—even the most supportive—must be put aside. When you put aside your memory of the past, there is no projection of future. Without past and future, your attention is fully present here, in this moment, regardless of what is appearing here. Even definitions of hell come from references to the past and hopes or fears for the future. When your mind is freed from definitions of any kind, you can easily and directly discover what is *really* here, rather than cling to any definition of what is here. Falling with surrender is naturally floating.

**So that you can tell** the unvarnished truth, the following points of inquiry are offered here for you alone. As spiritual seekers we know what we should think and feel. And we may even know, or remember, that the naked truth is silent open awareness. But this knowledge is worse than useless if there is no immediate, fresh, and ongoing direct experience of that knowledge. These questions have no "correct" answers. The questions are designed merely to direct your conscious attention into both the structure and substructure of your particular story and finally into the alive, silent awareness that is underneath all structures.

I recommend you give yourself time and space for these questions. You may want to write down the answers as you ask yourself the questions aloud. You may want to repeat all or particularly potent questions many times to discover unsuspected answers. All of the questions are open-ended. Answers to them can appear over time in different circumstances.

And you may find your own unique questions. If so, be aware that "why" questions lead to analysis, processing, and more mental activity. While this type of questioning is useful in many circumstances, in direct investigation "who" or "what" questions are more fruitful for fresh discoveries.

The more seriously you take both question and answer, the more is uncovered.

1. What is hell?
2. What does it mean about you that you find yourself in hell?
3. Who put you in hell?
4. Leaving behind all definitions, can you allow your attention to be *inside* the energy field or vibration of the experience of hell?
5. What is at the core of this experience?
6. Is there anything under that?
7. Under that?

When you have given yourself all the time you need, it may be helpful if you take a few moments to lie down and simply experience what has been evoked by both questions and answers. If you suspend all judgments and conclusions about any of your responses or any feelings evoked, what is here?

CHAPTER 8

# Offer of Redemption

To live truly full lives, we must be vigilant to how blinded we can be as we either fight or indulge our suffering. While inner states can be profoundly influenced by outer circumstances, we can unnecessarily continue a story of suffering long after the cause of the initial pain has passed and even when the vehicle of release from suffering is present. The experience of loss and the suffering that accompanies it usually initially obscure the possibilities of being released from the effects of that loss. We can become so fixated on our circumstance of misery that we overlook possibilities all around us.

In the larger metaphor of our teaching story, the divine redemption appears to the family as a stranger and is unrecognizable. So when this stranger makes an offering of salvation out of the blue, it seems too good to be true, and in our story the offer is categorically dismissed. The offering continues, but the family is certain of their irredeemable misfortune, which is the corollary to their earlier certainty of continuing good fortune. They ignore the offering and even view the continued persistence of the offer as harassment.

**In the midst** of the hell world of the Preventorium, in a moment of mysterious grace, I had felt the protective presence of love and comfort. I identified that presence as my guardian angel, and felt rescued from my suffering. Whenever I chose to look for that presence, I found it to be close by me. It was a redeeming force, but it couldn't save me from my subsequent choices. It couldn't save me from my "destiny" or my "karma." It couldn't save me from my own propensities to suffer.

I went to a Catholic school after I left the Preventorium and there I discovered the passionate Jesus. This discovery came with the offer of an institutional, conditional redemption. To secure my redemption I would have had to devote my life to Christ. I would have had to confess and then stop all my sinning. I would have had to pray certain prayers and attend certain rituals with a certain attitude. It was easy to reject those conditions. With my parents' willing support it was easy to recognize that I would rather play than pray; I had to learn my multiplication tables before I had the time to perform particular rituals. And the Episcopal church had much easier conditions to meet. I still felt Jesus loved me and watched over me, but I wasn't so sure I would meet him in heaven.

# Offer of Redemption

When I became a teenager, I discovered multiple pathways to escape the unhappiness I felt at home. But escape is not the same as redemption. In escaping the trials at home, I had to rely on my friends, alcohol, parties, schoolwork, and reckless sensual pleasure. Later I escaped through marriage and I escaped marriage through divorce. But these escapes were all only temporary releases, and they had to be continually replicated at least in some degree for their efficacy to return. True redemption saves you. It is singular and cannot be authentically replicated. It reveals the truth that you are safe now, with no possibility of true harm. It would be many years before I recognized an offer of true redemption.

The offer of redemption is the essence of the mystery of grace. In the darkest realms, with no hope and no possibility of hope, a hand is extended. From the perspective of hell, all hands offered are perceived as servants of hell itself. A helping hand can't be known to be the hand of redemption unless it is taken; yet in our teaching story and in our personal stories there are these hands. In our teaching story the helping hand is unbelievable to our family and is refused, as perhaps it is refused all too often in our own lives. Yet the helping hand is here.

Is it only in retrospect that we recognize the help that was offered all along?

Certainly in retrospect we can see that there have been hands that have pulled us out of many holes, and hands that have held us aloft. And we can give thanks for those hands. But what of the refused hands, the suspected hands, the resisted support?

When I look back at my life story, I recognize individuals and teachings that were always offering the way to redemption. At the time they appeared I might have even recognized their importance, yet there was something in me that could not fully accept it. In the late 1970s the Venerable Kalu Rimpoche came to Bolinas where Eli and I were living. We took Bodhisattva vows and empowerment initiations for Chenrezi, the Medicine Buddha, Mahakala, White Tara, and Green Tara. We performed prostrations to the Buddha, the Dharma, and the Sangha. We chanted in Tibetan and reveled in the particularly baroque and magical adornments the Tibetan tradition added to Buddhism. Eli was appointed head of the first Tibetan Dharma center in West Marin. We held daily five a.m. meditations in our home with the two other people who showed up, and had wonderful, phantasmagorical experiences.

As much as I loved the experience and valued the teachings, for me it was still just a wonderful experience. In many ways it was like the Catholic church experience I had had as a young girl, and after a year or so, Tibetan Buddhism became too much ritual and work for me. I moved on to a simpler version of Buddhism when I embraced Vipassana and Zen. In these traditions, as in my earlier experience of Christianity in general, I was never good enough. I could never sit still or long enough in Vipassana; my zazen practice was never pure enough or consistent enough.

I can see that luckily I did accept some of what was being offered by Buddhism and consciously recognized the support received. I was open to seeing and accepting more, but since it was escape I was still seeking, no offer of redemption could be final. No matter what moving or quieting experiences I had while meditating, I was consistently more faithful to the religion of my own suffering than to the offering of either the Christian or Buddhist religion. The practice of my own suffering kept its strong hold on my life.

When we are overly attached to the narration of the trials we may be suffering—*we* being we as individuals, we as families and communities, we as nations, and we as all living beings on the planet—we lose the capacity to recognize and investigate possible openings. Not all openings may lead to the solutions needed, but all can be investigated, and the more we are willing to investigate the openings that are here, the more possibilities there are for true solutions. The more we are open to investigate, the closer we are to redemption.

Our teaching story is simple. The problems facing our planet and our national and local communities are usually not so simple. But the principle remains the same in both simplicity and complexity. When we are bound to our stories of suffering, we are not free to see and receive creative help. We try the same old solutions, in varied dress with varied names, and for some period of time have a sense of resolution. But if the solution is ultimately false, the resolution is temporary.

What keeps us bound to our stories of suffering? Since the

stories reflect and generate pain, how is it possible that we habitually refer to them? Most likely we expect that if we retell the story of our fall from grace enough times we will discover why we fell, or how we fell, so as to never fall again. Uncovering *whys* and *hows* is quite useful, and yet the preoccupation with them can keep our attention fixated on the infinite possibilities of *why* and *how*. When we are fixated, our story of suffering becomes a macabre kind of entertainment. We become our own flagellators. So, in addition to the suffering directly caused by any actual reversal, we add our punishing mental replays as we futilely search for resolution through understanding.

Before we recognize our particular form of self-torture, the mental restimulation of our emotional pain is merely part of the package of the reversal. When we recognize this particular habit of mind, choice arises. When we become aware of choice, the mind is immediately more spacious. In the recognition of choice, victim mentality is loosened. We can hear our internal conversation and recognize the looping of certain recurring themes.

In my story, I had to recognize that for decades I had been telling different versions of the same woeful tale. If I experienced not having enough love, security, understanding, etc., then it was because I was deficient in some way. I would begin to mentally catalog my many deficiencies, along with promises to myself and vows to God to change and fix myself. If I experienced having enough of anything, I enjoyed the bounty only to the degree that I could stop waiting for the other shoe to drop. In my deepest evaluation of myself, I truly believed I didn't deserve enough. As an all-too-predictable result, rest and ease of being were held in check. I had to always be improving in some way, either to get something or to keep the dreaded demon of my persistent flawedness at bay.

When our attention is consumed by complaining, we overlook the way out of what we complain about. We spend the boon of our intelligence on rationalization and justification and overlook that within us which remains untraumatized by our traumas. Internally in all of us there is a silent door that is perpetually open. It is the door to redemption. All that is required is that we turn our attention inward and recognize that this doorway opens to spaciousness and peace.

When we can hear our internal conversation without judgment, we are outside the conversation. We are outside our particular inner mental and emotional war with events. The events may still be horrible with dire consequences, and we still may be the innocent victims of these events. But attention, now freed to some extent at least from involvement in events, is able to be aware of *what else is here.*

The cautionary-tale aspect of our teaching story is as important as the good news aspect. Stories of all kinds alert us to our capacity to ignore the door that has opened. Literature is filled with the tragedies of missed opportunities. Daily life on our planet proves that there are many for whom redemption never comes. There are many good, deserving people for whom it never comes. There are disasters that strike in an instant and as a result a person, or family, or world is finished. A tsunami wipes out a quarter of a million people and leaves millions homeless, a civil war continues so that generations know only loss and strife, a disease strikes mercilessly both the frail and the healthy, accidents of all kinds end the life story of those who moments before were flourishing and filled with the certainty of a future. This is the ruthless way of life. We try to make sense of it with our religions and metaphysics, and it relentlessly remains out of our control and beyond our understanding.

We also have stories that remind us that we can recognize such doors of redemption and walk through them. In religious literature we read of miraculous events that reveal oneness with the Father, or the emptiness of all phenomenal form. We read how seas were parted and that water can be made into wine. We read that all the temptations of the world, both beautiful and horrid, could not move a being committed to stand with truth. In our secular literature, the redemptions and revelations may have more ordinary dressings, but the result is just as extraordinary. An addict's life is turned around through the support of those who love him, a child is rescued from an abusive parent and saved from a life of torment. A loveless person discovers love with another person, with a pet, or—perhaps most miraculous of all—within himself or herself. In a poem, song, or story we can daily discover the redemptive possibilities all around us. To accept that radical, life-altering redemption can be possible is to open to its possibility.

With suffering and unredeemed tragedies all around us both globally and locally, how much more mysterious is the equally undeserved grace of an offer of redemption? The pure grace of the offer of redemption is demonstrated by the fact that the family in the teaching story did nothing to gain it. No work was done. The stranger appeared. The offer was made. And just as in reviewing certain instances of tragedy we often find signs that portended the tragedy—and if noted could have forestalled the tragedy—there are offerings of redemption present in our lives now. If our attention is free and open they needn't remain unseen.

In our teaching story, we can marvel at the odds of a stranger who knew the truth of the buried treasure taking the time and energy to search for a missing business acquaintance. Had an accident happened in his life or to someone close to him, had a new love interest or marriage occurred, or had any of a multitude of the normal distractions of daily life held his attention, this stranger could have gone his way without entering our story. And what luck that he is an honest man. A scoundrel could easily have stolen the treasure when he discovered the fate of his friend.

How easily, and in how many ways, what this stranger offered could have been lost before the offering. And yet here he is, against huge odds, simply telling the family, as well as telling us, the certain truth that will end the suffering.

He offers and offers and offers. The persistence of his offering is as marvelous as his willingness to devote a part of his life to the search for his friend. Even though he is rebuffed, he stays firm in offering. Truly, this blessed stranger is the defining grace of our story. He represents the angel of mercy, the manna from heaven, the miracle of hundreds of avoided mishaps that had the power to be tragedies. Without his appearance it is most likely that the family would continue its downward spiral. And yet his offer is meaningless until it is accepted.

We see in our teaching story, and perhaps in our lives, that quite often an offer presents itself to us cloaked in our own fears and certainties of helplessness. The family in our teaching story simply cannot see the stranger for who he is. By the time he enters our tale, their entire inner landscape is filled with proof of what won't be given back to them. Their reality doesn't allow them to perceive what to us, with our reader's perspective, seems obvious.

If you take the perspective of a reader of your own life, you can more easily discover both past and present offers of redemption. As long as you are completely identified with yourself as the victor or victim in your life, perspective is lost: the deeper vision is dimmed.

The concern of this book is actually not with the eventual good luck of this family. It is with your good luck. Our teaching story is a ploy to get your attention turned to what is being offered to us all. May it succeed.

**Inquiry is** an offer of redemption. It does not require any belief, or even any trust. Inquiry is investigation for yourself. Inquiring into what is hidden under the floorboards of your story of yourself reveals the true treasure of yourself.

We have myriad reasons why we can't inquire. We continue narrations that support our conviction that we have inquired in the past and found nothing. And still the invitation to inquire into the deepest levels *now*, as if for the first time, continues to be offered.

In this moment, if you skillfully assume that grace, or luck, or possibility is present in your life, offering you release from your suffering, will you accept? If the offer of redemption directs you to see underneath your story of suffering, to be naked to yourself, what do you find? If you find pain, are you willing to see and feel inside the pain? What is in the core, underneath it all?

POINTS OF INQUIRY:

1. Do you know the experience of being blinded by misfortune? So blinded that you cannot see the fortune that may actually be available?

2. Can you recall a time when you had no trust in the "friendliness of the universe"? Where do you feel that in your body?

3. Will you open to that feeling to discover what the deeper energy, or feeling, underneath it is?

4. When you open to that feeling or to the feeling of being helpless, without any story attached to the feeling, what is the experience?

# CHAPTER 9

# Cynicism, Refusal, Denial

When we cynically refuse an offer of redemption, we contribute to hardening the negative propensities of our mind. This hardening can be tragic. When we refuse what is life renewing, whatever our conscious or unconscious reasons, we die to life in some part. Knowledge of how we refuse and how we justify the refusal of the offering hand exposes the power of negative thinking and how it works to regenerate itself—often beyond the blow of the initial events of reversal.

When we find ourselves in horrible internal or external circumstances and we allow the cynical tendency of mind to prevail, we refuse the creative, positive outlook of mind. We become stuck in the mire of our own negativity, and any helping hand is viewed with suspicion or dismissed as superficial. We become too "smart" to receive the simplicity of true help.

When my parents sent me to the Preventorium, I felt they had condemned me to hell. In my fury at them, and given my young age, I could never consider that they had done it to try to help me. I had no clear notion of why I had been sent away, but I knew who had sent me. And I was blinded by my rage. When they made what was then a long trip from Clarksdale to Magee for visits on the weekends, I would hardly speak to them. The whole family would show up with smiles and big hellos. In pictures from that time I see Mama and Daddy, my new baby sister, and my older brother all standing in a cluster, and there I am, off to one side with a scowl on my face and my arms crossed over my chest.

When I see that picture now, I feel compassion for everyone in the picture. At the time I felt betrayed by everyone. There was no opening in my little heart to receive the love they offered. There was not even the willingness to open to enjoying their visit as a respite from the tedium of the daily schedule of the place.

Nihilistic, resigned thought process is the opposite of open discovery. In resignation there is an arrogant certainty that any effort is useless and that no help will come. This is a dangerous phase in the continuing dark night of hell. At this time it appears to the cynic, as it did to the mother in our teaching story, and to me in my story, that negative thinking is simply intelligence. Arrogance is certain: "I know what is real, and it is all bad news." For me at the Preventorium, I was simply certain that I had been abandoned by those I trusted and that all was lost. My particular display of refusal was anger and cynicism toward the offered hand in public, and anguished despair at night when alone in my bed.

In retrospect, I can see many hands offered and many refused in my life. When caught in the throes of any negative emotion, it's hard to even see—much less accept—the way out. I accepted the refuge of the bosom of Susie when I had felt my body disappearing, and I refused my family's visits to the Preventorium. I didn't think about either as choice. I was unaware of choice until many years later. Perhaps I was punishing my parents with my anger in a small act of suicide. I had no reason to punish Susie; she was there when I needed her, so I fell into refuge with her.

In our teaching story family, each member has become mired in their individual and collective suffering. The offer from the stranger appears to them as either gibberish or cruelty. By the time he appears, their worldview has hardened, and it is inconceivable to them that he could authentically offer release from their suffering. What could he know of their loss? Who is he to tell them that release is already here? In their arrogance of victimhood, they can only see aggressors and, astoundingly, feel taunted by the benevolence of this stranger.

I can remember first reading the words of Ramana Maharshi and responding deeply to them. Almost immediately, however, I thought to myself, "This is too simple for my complicated life." In my clinging to the complication of my suffering, I rejected the open hand offered in the words "Be still and know yourself."

By the time his words appeared in my life, I had become convinced that I was too complicated for easy solutions. I had plenty of experience that happiness came and then too quickly went. I never considered the possibility of a deeper happiness—my true nature—that was free of the bounds of appearing and disappearing. I could accept that such a nature may be true for enlightened ones, or saints, or simple folk, but I put myself in the fold of sophisticated, angst-ridden, doomed-to-suffer special ones. And, I am sad to say, I was proud of it. To my mind it proved that I couldn't be duped by a too easy access to happiness. I had outgrown all that. In truth, like our teaching family, I had stopped my emotional growth at cynicism. I had outsmarted myself.

Did our teaching family have a legitimate right to be suspicious about a stranger offering good news when they had so recently been educated about the ruthlessness of the universe? Yes, of course, and as a young child I had a reason to feel betrayed by my family when they sent me away to the Preventorium. The issue is how long we allow the right to suffer to dictate the continuance of suffering. When disaster or even mild disillusionment occurs, how long will we withhold ourselves from discovering what the universe is offering now, in the present time? If patterns of denial and refusal of what is being offered continue for years and then decades, these patterns become our very identity. The "sophistication" of recognizing the impersonal, ruthless nature of life becomes just as shortsighted and limiting as the childish assumption that all of life is designed to provide us with pleasure and happiness.

# Cynicism, Refusal, Denial

---

**When we** grow weary with our own sophistication, we often crave the innocence of earlier times. We equate childish viewpoints with innocence, and bounce between versions of resigned surrender and blind clear-sightedness.

The earlier times are innocent only in the way that the larval stage is innocent of the coming metamorphosis. And closed mindedness based on hurts from the past is not truly clear-sighted.

It is possible to recognize the pains that accompany life changes without closing our minds. It is possible to remove the stigma that pseudo-innocence puts on pain and loss, and meet pain and loss fully, eyes wide open. It is possible to consciously mature into whatever is awaiting with no idea of what that may be. And the possibility is available when we recognize what remains changeless when all else changes.

**The intelligence** of refusal or resistance—the intelligence to say no—is a mark of maturity. The intelligence to refuse what is unwanted or unneeded is sensible. It comes from a maturing, discerning mind. Even as infants we refuse. Refusal is a power, and to use it well is to be wise. Cynicism makes a religion of refusal. As all religions, it has a creed and dogma and a particular worldview. And just as all religions, it is founded on the desire to be free.

The cynic's practice is to discover what is or even what could be wrong with what is being offered by a stranger, in a loss, or through any internal or external event. The basic intention in finding what could be wrong is intelligent, but the practice of *searching* for what is wrong is self-defeating. As in other practices of any dogma, the practitioner becomes entwined in what—at its root—was originally there to set him or her free.

The blows that come to unquestioning innocence provide the ground for the religion of cynicism. The result is not the intended protection from false gods, pipe dreams, or snake oil salesmen. By the time cynicism has taken root, the result is a constricted life.

**At different times** in my life I have flirted with cynicism. Even now I recognize cynical patterns of thought as I scroll through the news from around the world. And I also notice that there is a degree of superiority alongside the cynical thoughts—a sense that it is my intelligence that gives rise to the smirk or the sarcastic *ha*. When I investigate the feeling under the protective cover of cynicism, I discover a pain. And when I stop protecting myself from that pain, I experience it fully. When I don't follow the thoughts that justify the cynicism, I feel the rawness of being consciously human in a world that does not conform to my ideals. In being willing to directly experience the rawness, I no longer avoid the reality of false gods and betrayals, and I no longer try to protect myself from the pain of that reality. In that moment my mind is open, and even if the pain is still present, I am at peace.

I notice that in being willing to fully let the hurt be, there may be some residue of pain, but there is no longer a smirk. I notice that I am both aware of the futility of much of humankind's endeavors, and also the beauty and mystery of the entire display. I am not separate from any of humankind. Many of my own endeavors will never come to fruition, and underneath there remains a beautiful mystery at play. My attention is returned to open curiosity, with no need to either deny or confirm what is in front of me. At such a moment of surrender both yes and no are freed from the function of protecting me from pain and can subsequently arise from natural intelligence.

**Empathy** with the sudden loss of innocence the family experiences in our teaching story allows us to understand the arising of cynicism. The story doesn't let us know exactly how long it took for cynicism to take root, but it is clear that it took some time. Surely we know this for ourselves. It's not the first blow that makes us wince or fight back or cower.

Fighting back, running, or hiding are intelligent responses to abuse. Yet if we perceive the world itself as abusive, fighting and hiding only serve to limit us. To retreat from the world and all its accompanying noise is sweet and necessary for deep rest. But if our retreat is in actuality cowering in denial of the world or fighting back with cynical armoring, we only suffer more. Our own minds become the abusive agent.

**When I look back** at the time of the Preventorium and the hardening of my heart against my family, I recognize how that hardening colored all following family events until decades later, when I was finally ready to face the pain I had hardened myself against.

There were many other areas of my life where I remained open and curious. With my friends, with the possibility of my future, with life in general I was open to discovery. With my family and later others who represented my family to me—what we called significant others—I was distrusting and certain that they would only inflict more wounds. I found the proof of their untrustworthiness whenever their behavior conflicted with my ideas of how they should behave. The proofs accumulated until our relationships were states of siege, with occasional bursts of battle. No one could ever show enough love to make me know they really loved me. I couldn't begin to see them as distinct people with lives and problems of their own. They were all about me.

My parents and most of my long-term significant others wouldn't play my habitual game of war. They lived their lives as they saw fit, not as I did. My aggression, alternating with my melancholy, was unattractive to all. When I discovered that my displays of wrath or sadness had no effect on their lives, I only became more melancholy. My suffering became my identity. All I could hope for was escape.

# Cynicism, Refusal, Denial

My story opened with this desire of escape. And I found escape in many forms throughout my adolescence, throughout college and my first marriage, through change of lifestyle, through accumulation of knowledge and experience, through experimentation with danger, and through success. It was not until in the years before I met Papaji and especially in meeting him that I began to realize that seeking escape had become the source of my suffering. Attempted escape from the possibility of hurt alternating with theatrics around the inevitable hurts of life had become the dogma of my religion of emotional hurt. The more I tried to repress the hurt I felt inside, the more my life was fixated on it. Like all dogmas, it had ensnared me with the promise of salvation. I had never considered being cynical of my dogma, or even been aware that cynicism had a hold on my life at all. But it did.

As long as I found escapes from whatever was tormenting me, I could avoid the hard heart I secretly felt to be the inner me. The hardening around my heart was a result of cynicism regarding my capacity to truly love and be loved, my refusal to meet fully the pain of reversal of fortune, and the denial of the open, clear innocence alive under it all.

When you examine your story, do you find parallels? We each have unique experiences of life as a whole and of the particular events of our own lives. Yet under the surface events of lives that appear even radically different, there are patterns and habits that are quite similar. The questions that follow are meant to assist you in discovering what cynicism, refusal, and denial have looked like in your life story. Most important, they are here to support you in discovering what your life story is teaching.

POINTS OF INQUIRY:

1. Have you ever felt lost in negativity? If so, are you aware of indulging negative thoughts and emotions (obsessively replaying the causative factors)?
2. Do you recall gathering consensual opinion among others to support your suffering? What was the result?
3. Can you recall that emotion now?
4. If so, will you directly meet that emotion simply as energy, without repressing it through dissociation or indulging it by continuing the narrative of the event that evoked it?
5. Are you aware of the power of choice in either continuing or stopping the narrative of any particular story line?
6. Start a familiar story in your mind, and in the middle of a sentence, simply stop.
7. What is the result?

# CHAPTER 10

# The Right Question

At night, in my cold steel bed at the Preventorium, I prayed. Of course I had only a child's notion of prayer, but I used it with ferocity. I didn't have the maturity to question why or how I had gotten into this situation, I just knew I wanted out desperately. I prayed to Jesus, to my idealization of the Jesus who must love me and who could save me. One blessed night, maybe halfway between sleeping and waking, I became aware of a soft and radiant presence offering deep comfort. Jesus had sent my guardian angel to be by my side! I was in wonder but also in acceptance, since the presence felt both natural and familiar. I allowed myself to be held in the folds of love, and I began to rest.

Each night I communicated with my guardian angel. She was very real to me, yet only over time did I have a mental image to go with my feeling of her presence. The form she took in my mind was the one I had seen in a picture of a beautiful, all-loving guardian angel watching over two little children who are being threatened by an approaching storm. I felt completely at ease in her presence, and knew without a doubt that she would be by my side whenever I needed her. Perhaps she took Mammy's place, since—unlike Mammy—she was with me anywhere, anytime.

Much later in my life I had more sophisticated explanations for what had occurred, but the unvarying truth—whatever the explanation—was that through this experience I was lifted from desolation into solace and consolation. I could look out of my eyes and begin again to experience the fun and adventure of my life rather than being fixated on my inner trials.

Everything got better. I could eat more, and I played effort-lessly with the other children, and then one day my family came to get me. I don't even remember that day, since I had already been rescued when my angel protector made herself known to me. Life was easier in every way when I got back to Clarksdale. Since I was not so focused on what I wasn't getting, I was able to naturally love my baby sister.

I had missed some months of first grade, so my parents put me in the local Catholic school, as the classes were smaller, and I was likely to get more attention there. There was much that was terrible about the school. The nuns, with their long black woolen habits, their strange smells, and their protruding starched wimples, looked and often behaved like bad witches.

Since I was an Episcopalian, the nuns considered me lost to God; nevertheless I still had to attend the morning catechism class. What a surprise that I loved it. I was introduced to a passionate Jesus, surrounded by passionate followers willing to die horrible deaths just to be reunited with him in heaven. Here was a Jesus with a heart bleeding from all the love he had for all of us (me!). And here was his beautiful, eternally pure mother, serene with her open arms offering protective care. The statues and stories of the saints completed the holy family I now spent time with every day. I felt that I was meeting my real family. I felt I was home. I was very happy.

When I began fashioning little shrines to Mary and Jesus around our house, Mama and Daddy soon realized that all was not as they had expected it to be. When I asked to be able to go to mass with my Catholic cousins, they allowed it a few times. With dismay, however, they soon saw that they might be promoting an eccentric by keeping me in the Catholic school, so by second grade I was in Clarksdale's public school.

I conformed to their wishes and reined in my religious fervor. Only later did I realize how I paid for that conformity, but still I had my guardian angel, and still I loved Jesus with all my heart. My prayer had been answered. Grace had appeared in an emotionally starved life and had nourished a shriveling heart. Though I had many more moments of pure love as well as long periods of suffering awaiting me in the future, though I had decades filled with failed challenges before I could be steadfastly true to the mystery of love that had penetrated my suffering, I happily no longer felt myself to be totally adrift and alone.

Hidden Treasure

---

**In our teaching story,** it is the youngest child who still displays enough innocence, which is open-mindedness, to finally ask the right question. Such a simple, obvious question, and yet it penetrates the complex mental fog of cynicism. "Will you show us where the treasure is?"

The simplest questions reveal the simple and undeniable truth underneath all our complex mental gyrations. When we first become aware that we *are*, there is wonder and that wonder is met with intelligence. We are, but what are we? Looking up at the stars, discovering our own and other bodies, becoming conscious in sickness and in health all contribute to our wonderment and our intelligent capacity both to question and to formulate answers. The great questions lead to great discoveries. The feedback loop of great question and great discovery leads to more and expanded capacity to question and to greater discoveries.

**Over millennia,** in countless ways, our questioning has revealed both the light at the end of the tunnel and the dead end, since as human animals we mostly discover through trial and error. Those who have gone before us are sometimes able to pass on what they have discovered, and sometimes no matter how many times something has been discovered, we have to discover it freshly for ourselves. We can be warned away from or invited into, but for us to truly know a thing we have to taste it ourselves.

Because this procedure takes time, we rightfully rely on others for information about this life experience we share. We have scientists of every discipline, artists of all kinds, philosophers in all fields, and explorers and mapmakers of our physical world to share their discoveries with us. We learn from and marvel at it all. It informs us, entertains us, and protects us. We find stimulation and comfort in the knowledge available to us.

And, yet, until we ask of *ourselves* the most basic, the most simple of questions, we do not know ourselves directly. The journey between the unquestioning wonder of initial self-discovery and the deepest self-realization is an endless journey until closed in an instant by the right question.

**Our teaching story** shows how misery and degradation can pollute the natural clarity of mind to such an extent that the simplest and most essential question is beyond reach. At the point of the appearance of the stranger, the entire family has succumbed to their particular versions of negative intelligence. They have succumbed, not surrendered. They are defeated, not open. The barrenness of their lives is their reality and a way out is not considered. In their defeat they even defend their misery against the stranger's offer. They are attached to the stagnation and continual looping of mind activity as reality. We may easily wonder at their abject ignorance, but if we read the family as our human family, and each of the members of the family as each of us, then we are closer to seeing that we too often defend what contributes to our misery. Strangely, we develop the habit of perversely fighting to keep our victim identity. Seeing this common form of ignorance is the first step to opening the mind to unknown possibility. Seeing deeper into the structure of our suffering is an invitation to grace.

And in a moment of grace, the right question appears. The right question naturally brings forth the right answer or at the least clears the space for discovery. The stranger could never satisfy the family's wrong questioning. They ask him, "Why are you taunting us?" and he answers, "I am not taunting you. I can help you." In their blindness, which is our blindness, they had stubbornly wanted only the answer to their question about his reasons for taunting them. The stranger can easily answer the right question: "Will you show us?" Space opens. The waters part. The way is clear. The matter settled.

When we are children, our cognitive functions are usually not sophisticated enough to formulate an essential question. And if we ask, "Who am I?" we are answered with our particular name, or with our relationships ("You are Daddy's little girl . . ."). When we are adults, our cognitive functions have become so sophisticated that we overlook the simple questions for the more complex. "Why is this happening to me?" "What do I need to do to make something happen or not happen?" "Who did this to me?" are just samples of the many questions we ask that can only have multilayered, complex answers. Assuredly, complex answers reflect the complexity of many situations and accordingly have merit. Nonetheless, they can only take attention into the maze of versions upon versions of stories. They can never lead to the limitless, storyless, answer that is the naked truth of oneself.

With even a childish prayer for help, the mind can open to the assurance of ultimate protection. This life-enhancing presence may be named guardian angel, or Self, or God, but all names are more complicated than the experienced reality of the presence.

When we repeatedly ask questions that only cause us to suffer more, we spend our time going in circles. When we persistently ask "Why? Why? Why?" we continue the useless habit of chasing our own tails. Fixating on who is to blame, what we should or should not have done, or could or could not have done, keeps our attention on the problem rather than the solution.

The right question is an example of innate intelligence asserting itself, even if apparently for the wrong reasons. In our story, the young child wants the stranger to stop bothering the family with talk of treasure. The talk of treasure is painful to them all, as they are aware only of their lack. They all just want the stranger to go away. Nevertheless the right question appears. "If he's so sure it's here, why not get him to find the treasure?" Although framed as only a strategy to get rid of the stranger, the question actually serves to break the logjam of the family's denial of possibility. The opening is confirmed with the stranger's surprise answer of "I will."

Throughout our lives the conscious turning points have followed deep questioning. "What do I want?" "What is the meaning of it all?" "What is my life about?" "What am I doing?" "What should I do?" "Why am I suffering?" "How do I change my life?" "How do I find happiness?" "Where is God?" "Who am I?"

The list may be endless, but when certain pivotal questions are asked, the question itself turns the mind's attention to the answer. The right question is never satisfied by our hackneyed habitual answers. The Indian sage Ramana Maharshi faced a time of trial in his teenage years by asking, "Who dies?" The depth of his inquiry led to his profound awakening to that which cannot die. He advised his disciples to ask, "Who am I?" When sincerely and fully asked, this question finally reveals boundless conscious awareness as one's true identity. The question reveals the consciousness that is present in but not limited to the body of any particular questioner.

If we are willing to ask the right question, the answers are here. If we are willing to stop our mental activity to ask the *essential* questions, discovery is revealed.


POINTS OF INQUIRY:

1. What do you want?
2. If you had that, what would it give you?
   (Repeat #2 until your answer reveals what you truly want, in the deepest part of yourself.)
3. Where have you looked for it?
4. What is present in the core of your being, needing no story or emotion or sensation for its reference point?

CHAPTER 11

# Discovery

When the right question is asked and attention is turned toward discovery rather than loss and negativity, the perception of inner space expands. What we were blind to an instant before is suddenly obvious. Inner and outer forces can thwart the approach to discovery, but at the actual moment of discovery there is only surprising revelation.

All stories have discovery as their pivotal point. After discovery the world is no longer flat, the moon not so far away after all, and perhaps even a deadly disease is vanquished. Not all discoveries are fortuitous, of course. A friend can be revealed to be an enemy; what we believe to be true can be discovered to be a lie. We can discover that disease is taking our life away, or that we have already lost what we most love. We discover some hard truths in tragedy, and we discover joyous perennial wisdom in renewal and birth. We are conscious, intelligent creatures, and our lives are filled with discoveries of all kinds.

Our teaching family has discovered the good luck of buried treasure, surely an archetypical dream discovery. Their material trials are over, and they rightfully feel saved. As it is a teaching story designed to demonstrate the truth of the bounty at the core of our beingness, we leave our family just at the moment of their momentous discovery.

If they have gained some wisdom from their troubles, they will be prudent with how they use their windfall. Perhaps they will feel compassion toward the suffering of others. Maybe they will even take the opportunity of their trials—and release from those trials—to investigate essential questions of life and identity. We can know that if they remain oblivious of how quickly life circumstances can be altered, they will have more hard lessons ahead.

Theirs is a miraculous discovery, and yet far from the discovery of discoveries the teaching aspect of the story reveals. The real point of their discovery is not the recovery of material wealth, but the fact that it was there *all along*, under their feet. We hope and believe that material wealth will save us, redeem us, as we hope for emotional and mental wealth. And certainly, having enough of all forms of wealth restores a sense of fundamental security. We don't need to demean the importance of enough (and the pleasure of more than enough) material, emotional, and mental provisions to realize that none of those is enough for lasting fulfillment.

Even if the family members are wise with their material bounty, what of their true, inner wealth? We can't know if they have any inkling of what "inner wealth" even means, but we can tell the truth about our own story. Are you aware of your inner wealth? Is it hidden away, even forgotten, or is it being explored to discover if there are limits?

One of the most important discoveries of my life was primarily negative, and yet because of it I was brought to the absolutely essential discovery of my life story. By the late 1980s I was living a very good life. Eli and I had moved from Bolinas to Mill Valley. We were living in a wonderful little house with a manageable mortgage. We both had fulfilling work, and although our relationship still had its trials, we recognized each other as life partners. We loved the community we lived in, and we loved each other. And yet . . .

There was a longing that continued to return. It let me know that however my life looked and felt, however far I had come from my earlier discontent, something deep inside remained unfinished. I couldn't have articulated *what* was unfinished, since nothing in particular was wrong. Often I would ignore the longing, or categorize it as part of my basic neurotic mental/emotional fixation.

At that time in my life I was certain that I had discovered all that I needed to know to live a happy, useful life. I had explored many different spiritual and secular paths, and I had discovered many useful tools to appease the yearning in my heart. I knew to dance or walk in nature if I felt stressed. I knew to meditate to calm my overactive mind. I knew to leave "my" life at the door when helping those who were troubled in some way. I knew that direct and honest communication with my partner was required for a mature relationship. I knew to vote with my conscience and heart at both elections and shops. I knew a lot, but I didn't know what the longing wanted.

Finally I was willing to know that I didn't know. Initially this evoked negative feelings. I *thought* I *should* know. I *wanted* to know. I wanted the uncomfortable feeling in my chest to be cured by all that I knew and practiced. After a brief and miserable period of resisting the truth, I opened my mind to the fact that once again—when I told the most naked truth—I was aware of longing for what I could not even name. I surrendered all pride of accomplishment to the truth that at a fundamental level I remained unfulfilled.

As I had prayed for rescue forty-odd years before, I now prayed to know the truth. Was the truth the glimpses I had had of perfection and beauty, or was the truth the drudgery of life, with glimpses of unbounded love simply a mechanism of brain chemistry to assist this body in getting through life? I didn't know the answer, but I prayed that if there was someone who did know the truth, I might meet and learn from that someone.

# Discovery

<hr/>

**It was a different order** of prayer from the childish plea I had offered up to Jesus. If the truth was that we are doomed creatures of birth-procreation-death, designed only to continue the species in a mechanical universe, I was ready to face that reality. If the truth was something more, I wanted to know that. I wasn't looking for a guru or a savior; I was looking for a true teacher.

Within a year of recognizing that I was ready to face the truth and that I needed help in knowing where and how to look, I met my teacher. Surprising to me he was a guru, and even more surprising I had to travel to India to meet him. I had always scoffed at the sentimental, incense-laden devotee relationship to the "guru." I was certain that my Western sophistication put me way beyond what a guru could show me. I wasn't seeking escape in mindless devotion, and I had no patience with name changing and affecting Eastern traditions as a lifestyle. I was wrong. My so-called sophistication and certainty became insignificant with the appearance of my teacher.

Eli met Papaji first. The letters he wrote to me while visiting this remarkable man were vibrating with love and insight. He wrote me that this man, H. W. L. Poonja, was the real thing. He wrote that he was coming back to get me so that I could meet what we had been searching for our entire lives.

Soon I found myself at the bank of the Ganga (Ganges), face-to-face with an enormous force of presence and energy. In the first instant of meeting him, I knew he was the answer to my prayer. He met us at the door of the small house he rented in Haridwar. As the door opened, I was greeted with an authentic and robust "Welcome, come in!" His deep eyes were flashing with intelligence and joy. I fell in love.

I had no idea what was to follow, but I knew to pay close attention. What was to follow was the discovery of my lifetime. Unknowable to me at the time, the discovery I experienced in his presence, through his grace and guidance, was the opening that naturally led to the profound, truly indescribable shift that finally put me right side up in my life. Meeting him, listening to him, and being with him precipitated a discovery that appeared as a thunderclap in my mind and that is still, quietly now, exploding within me twenty years later.

When I asked my teacher how I could discover the truth—at the time I phrased it as how I could discover freedom—he told me to discover who I am. When I asked him, "How?" he told me to stop everything. He told me to keep still.

Without really understanding how keeping still could answer my questions, I followed his suggestions. As I took his instruction deeper into my consciousness, I recognized how *stop* was a very threatening word to me. I imagined that if I kept still, and stopped everything, I would certainly regress and lose all my spiritual accomplishments. I did not want to end up being the person I was back in Clarksdale, Mississippi. I was afraid that if

I really stopped, I might have no desire to take care of myself or others. Finally I recognized that in my understanding, to stop meant to die. I was afraid to die. After some useless internal discussions, I did realize that while I might die here in this place, it wasn't likely. I recognized that the fear of death kept me from examining what was here if I truly did keep still. If I stopped searching for anything or hiding from anything, what would I discover?

He told me that what I was looking for was closer than my breath or heartbeat and that it was always here. He said that only what is continuously here could truly be called real. He told me to discover what was real. I listened to him and stopped following the thoughts that arose about my future. I stopped thinking about who I was and what I needed. I was still. Astoundingly, I discovered that the seemingly continuous narrative of my thoughts was not continuous after all. I saw clearly that whoever or whatever I thought myself to be changed with passing thoughts and definitions. My definitions of myself were not continuous and therefore not real.

When I withdrew my attention deeper and *closer* than any thought of myself, or my world, or my accomplishments, or my needs, I discovered conscious space. Space that was conscious! Conscious space that in truth had always been the background of all my different thoughts. Was it continuous? He advised me to find out for myself. I began my investigation by keeping my attention on where thoughts arose from rather than following them out into thought streams.

Thoughts appeared and disappeared, and conscious space remained, regardless of the appearance or disappearance of those thoughts. Definitions and descriptions and stories of dazzling variations all had beginnings and endings. I realized that conscious space was the generator and the receiver of all. I discovered that conscious space was both silent and aware. I was conscious of myself as this silent, aware space.

I discovered myself to be inseparable from whatever appeared in consciousness (body, thoughts, emotions, states of being) and at the same time independent of all forms. I discovered that the duality of our everyday perceptions was enclosed in and penetrated by the unity of conscious space.

Silent, empty, and full too, I found myself to be continuous awareness paradoxically both finding myself and recognizing I had always known myself. This startling—and yet obvious!—discovery was infused with the purest love I had ever experienced. I had loved people and places and objects of beauty, but this love loved with no constraints or needs. I found myself as love in both subject and object.

In the first days and weeks of this astounding discovery, my attention would vacillate between sublime rest in its home and agitated attempts to define or control what was being revealed. It is one of the aims of our brain, after all, to make sense of our world. When I followed my habit of trying to *think* what was happening, I found only confusion and denial. When my thoughts took precedence I would feel a mild panic at losing what a moment before had seemed impossible to lose. I would think, "Where is it now? How have I lost it?" And then I would remember Papaji's voice: "Stop. Be still. Recognize who you are." With this encouragement I could stop my habit of searching. Released from seeking to find anything, I found only spacious love.

**Finally I became aware** of a distinct moment of choice: I could follow thoughts or I could be still. I could identify with reality as generated by the thought process, or I could identify with open, spacious awareness. It was a moment of fear as well as choice. It was a choice between the apparent security of *knowing* through my evaluations of reality and *discovering* through opening to reality. Knowing through thinking generated a wary illusion of safety, but at this point that pseudosecurity felt deadening and unsatisfying. Discovering was my choice. Is my choice.

**I was familiar** with the horror of brainwashing. I had been brainwashed as a child to see people with dark skin as inferior. I had been brainwashed to believe that eternal happiness could be found in finding the right man. I had been brainwashed to think I could achieve everlasting fulfillment by doing some magical "right" thing. Brainwashing is exclusion and requires keeping contradictory information out of consideration. The choice I was making was to open my mind to all.

It didn't seem possible when I thought about it. In fact it wasn't possible when I thought about it. Thoughts demand closing attention to one thing in favor of another. Normally when we are unable to choose which thought to favor, we become confused or "cognitively dissonant." We then usually desperately seek a thought that will deliver congruence with our learned view of reality.

I could not find a thought that would support fully opening my mind to all. I could not find a thought that condoned stopping thoughts. Opening was only possible in suspending reliance on any thought as accurate. I was willing. At the same time I also felt great fear of the possible consequences. I discovered that the willingness to open to what is unknown—and even beyond knowing—is a choice even in the midst of great fear.

What I discovered was not static or dry in any way. How to explain a silence that encloses and saturates the universe? I had read books and accounts about great beings' enlightenment, and I had imagined what that enlightenment must be. In an instant this discovery erased all comparisons of states and degrees of selfhood. I found silent awareness in this form called "me" and also recognized that when this form is long gone, silence, the conscious substance of life—undiminished by any loss—remains. Without the penetration of life animation, there is no form; yet when the form is finished (or when life animation is finished with the form) life still is.

Realizing and experiencing silent awareness as my own self

released a flood of life affirmation. There was a retreat of the fear of death, since life remains after "I" die, and above all I am life. There was laughter that rolled on and on, with tears of bliss and wonder. All questions and all answers were swallowed whole in the direct experience of being conscious of myself as consciousness itself.

**And I wasn't brain-dead,** or insensate, as I had feared I might be in the moment before surrender. There was a geyser of personal and global insights as my prior knowledge of life was silenced. There was the lucidity of pure sensual experience that found fulfillment in whatever the senses perceived. The exalted blissful state of self-recognition lasted some time, and when the state of bliss passed there was no longing or regret or sense of losing anything at all. *I am* was revealed to precede all states, to penetrate all states, and to remain when all states pass away.

There was no question of maintaining anything or keeping anything. Simply being, and being conscious that being *is* conscious, was the fulfillment. The natural surrender of my seeking mind opened windows of insight daily and even hourly. After leaving Haridwar, I wrote Papaji at least every day, and he answered with beautiful letters of encouragement and confirmation. I was deeply happy and didn't need anything more. Not needing anything more prepared the field of my mind for the lightning bolt that appeared out of the blue one night as Eli and I sat together, reveling in our good luck.

It was some weeks after my visit to Papaji had ended and we were in California, where Eli was leading a group at Esalen. In a moment of love and joy with each other and together appreciating the astounding grace of having met our true teacher, the world as I had known it stopped. When it started again (there was no time involved) I was free. Free of myself as form and free of myself as anything separate from any form. Free of myself as either form or formless. Free of ego and free of egolessness. Free of unenlightenment and free of enlightenment. Fulfillment was here with no search or searcher needed. The story of past suffering had no meaning or power in this instant. Peace and love. Blessed moment, blessed life, all was truly well.

I looked at Eli and saw we were the same self even in all our differences. Differences and sameness were parts of the wholeness of self. The war between *different* and *same* came to an end. The laughter that poured out was the only description I could make.

To this day, I can only say that from that moment there has been no lack of resolution and fulfillment. There have been negative states as well as positive. There has been grief as well as joy. There have been trials, and there have been defeats, but nothing has dislodged the certainty that who I am includes all.

And it had always been here. I could look through my life and re-create my personal story, and from the perspective of consciousness recognize myself as pure silent awareness always having been here. The only difference was that now I included myself *as* awareness along with the objects (I, you, events, emotions, etc.) in awareness.

I could think without being tyrannized by thoughts. I could tell my story without needing it to be anything other than another display of life in form. I recognized that same display of life in all forms, both beautiful and horrid. I recognized that same display in all emotions, in all recoiling and all embracing. I recognized the uncontrollability as well as the undeniability of life awake to itself, and I fell on my knees in gratitude and wonder.

**This discovery** did not go unnoted by my teacher—my guru. He was very happy. He supported and confirmed my discovery and always challenged me to more fully, more deeply, more completely discover more. He would say, "See if you can find an end." He also told me that this discovery was so precious that the mind would try to steal it, and as a good thief it would use all its skills and powers to own this precious treasure. He said the mind would be as a wolf in sheep's clothing and that constant vigilance was required.

There were many more discoveries awaiting me as I began to recognize the mandate and force of my thinking mind. There were great challenges waiting and great humbling as I discovered the truth of my guru's warnings. My states ranged from high to low and my ideas about myself paraded in flat deflation and absurd inflation. Yet in both the worst and the best of times, silent awareness, *aware of itself,* remained the ground of being. Present in all, unmoving, and radiant.

"My" discoveries are not mine, of course. They are absolutely fresh and authentic but not new or unique. My moment of awakening was not the rescue or the kind of treasure I was looking for. It did not bestow magic powers or protection from pain. It did not elevate me from being a human being, or save me as a human being from my genetic tendencies. It blessedly did reveal what needed no rescue to be free and what needed no magic power or freedom from humanness to experience life fully and freely in love.

It was both more and less than I was looking for. The simplicity and depth of being can only be diminished or elevated by the thinking mind. In direct experience that simplicity and depth overwhelm all mental attempts to calibrate in any direction whatsoever. It is. I am. More than can be known; all that is known.

I have always failed at accurately describing my self-discovery, although this failure is inseparable from the beauty and the profundity of the discovery. It will not be caught and held by words. It has remained free and alive, and undeniable, while I have blissfully attempted to define or describe it.

There is peace and bliss, but what is most essential about this discovery is its pure *aliveness*. In a completely real sense, it is not something that *happened* to me; it is the discovery of who I am. It is simultaneously the background, foreground, and middle ground. It is pure life that is constant, regardless of what is born or what dies.

**It knows itself** because its substance is consciousness. It finds itself in all form and in formlessness too. It is the whole and in all aspects of that wholeness. And yet it is both more and less than these descriptions. It is the same now as when it first proclaimed itself before I knew my name as *I am*. Whatever events and changes have occurred in this form, none has touched the alive presence of myself. The body has aged and will continue to age; experiences deepen the experience of life; expansion and contraction appear and disappear; emotions and equanimity, like yin and yang, flow into and out of each other.

In the most fundamental sense, it was the thinking process that had to stop to discover that *I am* is prior to any thought or name of myself. Abstractly this may be seen as obvious and therefore inconsequential, but in actuality—because of our attachments to and belief in our thoughts as reality—this discovery was revelatory beyond measure. Whether this recognition of oneself as consciousness is found to be a function of the brain or proof of a supraintelligence is not my concern. I am concerned only with the discovery and the effect it has had on my life since.

The "validity" of the experience in any terms—scientific, spiritual, religious—is untouched by the truth of it in my life. Likewise, I have no problem with how anyone else chooses to define or diagnose it.

Lasting fulfillment can only come when discovery is of the endless wealth of the overflowing core of oneself—*silent conscious awareness*. We all know the pleasure of attainment and the pain of grief when we lose what we have attained. The invitation here is to recognize the treasure that cannot be attained because it is already here. It is the same treasure that is revealed when we consciously lose everything. When we are willing—for a moment at least—to stop keeping any thought of our world and ourselves alive. What lasts is not anything that is subject to the law of change. Silent awareness is aware of changes, even inseparable from changes, and yet free of changes.

We know at least the initial outcome of our teaching family's discovery, and you know much of my discovery, but what of yours? Has there been significant, life-altering discovery, either sudden or over time? If you step back from your story, are you able to tell the truth about what is needed for this story named *I* (attached to whatever name you presently answer to) to reach resolution?

You may or may not practice praying, but yearning or longing for resolution can be seen as a kind of praying. What do you yearn for? Can you open your mind so that the yearning itself, independent of what it may be attached to, can direct your attention to possibilities of discovery and resolution?

POINTS OF INQUIRY

1. Are you willing to stop looking outside yourself for this moment of discovery?

2. What is discovered deep inside the core of yourself when there is no story of unfulfilled desires attached?

3. Are you willing to stop and check several times during the day to see if this in the core is present until you know *without a doubt* it is always here?

4. Are you willing to be unbound by stories, or names, or history?

5. Are you willing to be naked to yourself?

# Part Three

# CHAPTER 12

# Open End

Just as all stories end, all lives end; and in a life—or even a day—emotions, thoughts, and sensations end. Anything that has a beginning has an end. Clearly this is both factual and obvious, yet the seeming starkness of the fact causes it to be overlooked, denied, and fought. The recognition of and peace with endings is a mark of all-too-rare maturity. The necessary recognition of the inevitability of endings is preparation for the mind to open to the realization of limitlessness. Not the limitlessness of a thing or a body or even a universe: the limitlessness of pure no-thingness, limitless space.

Our teaching story ends with the beginning of renewed prosperity for the family. That story will end someday too, even if the ending is generations away. My story and your story have had many endings and hopefully will have many more until the finality we name *death*.

It is the certainty, even if denied, of an ending that gives our individual and universal stories their immediacy and poignancy. Some endings are abrupt and seem to make all that came before meaningless and worthless. A young life taken inexplicably defies understanding. And some are natural and graceful and resolve all that came before, naturally preparing the way for the next cycle of life experience. An aging parent or grandparent seen with the newest addition to their family evokes a sense of the rightness of things.

If we become sentimental about the preciousness of our story, we display infantile behavior when the inevitable end is perceived. We rage, sob, or crawl into a pseudococoon of some kind—drugs, alcohol, mind-numbing activities, etc. If we are sober in our recognition of endings, our stories can be viewed as reflections of our particular love affairs with life. Not always smooth and easy by any means and sometimes genuinely tragic, but worth it all the while.

**Back in** my early adolescence I lived and breathed stories, and I was melded to the story appearing as *me*, Toni Roberson, as were people around me with their stories. I formed my different versions of *me* by closely following how other stories took their form. I studied movie stars and the roles they played. I watched the adults and older children in our small town and listened to their dialogue. The children in our neighborhood would sometimes put on Saturday "performances" as we played at being different characters. (My most memorable role was Salome in the dance of the seven veils.) I lost myself in both cheap books and good literary works as I pieced together my *me* character. This is common to us all in our different ways. It takes time and imitation and experimentation as well as genetic affinity to build a coherent, multilayered character.

As a young girl I began to work on my perceived ugliness. I subscribed to *Seventeen* magazine and studied it faithfully every night. I learned to wear makeup, bras, and girdles. This started when I was only in the seventh grade. Then I learned to smile at people and make friends. I didn't feel so lonely and, as long as I got positive feedback, I didn't feel so ugly. It did take work. Hair rollers every night, dealing with pubescent acne, and keeping the secret of my family's alcoholism required all my vigilance. But after a while I had good girlfriends who were interested in the same beautifying and popularity building, and we were having fun.

Periods of respite from my deep lack of self-regard always came to an end. Yet in my immaturity, I repeatedly thought the latest way I had found to handle life would last forever. When my adolescent strategies no longer worked, I was shocked into an altogether different realm of maturation. All my later attempts at handling life—perpetually revolving around keeping my ugliness and loneliness at bay—would ultimately end, and each time was a shock. Each shock was unwanted in its time, but each shock helped weaken the structure of my *me*. Each helped reveal the capacity of *life* to ruthlessly and impersonally disintegrate the latest version of *me*.

When I recognized my relative powerlessness in the face of the power of life with its unknowable future, I was humbled. At first the humbling was a humiliation and simply a part of my sad story. A part I needed to "work on." When I stopped resisting the humbling, it became a beautiful opening. It was the beginning of surrender. I became conscious of how I was collecting certain aspects from the events of life, and life's reversals, to feed my personal story of suffering. I slowly began to acknowledge to myself that at least some of that suffering must be unnecessary. I began to question the previously unquestioned legitimacy of my thoughts about myself.

I remember a particular moment in the midst of sobbing in misery (I was in my thirties by then) when I realized that in a strange and unsatisfying way I was taking some pleasure from my emotional suffering. In that instant I chose to look more closely into my subtle masochism. As a result of that shocking revelation, I began to deeply reflect on my life story. Finally I discovered the thread that had held my tragic story in place.

When I examined my days at the Preventorium, I *knew* my parents were victimizing me. It was painful, and there was no pleasure at all. And then I was rescued by my vision of an angel, and there was exquisite bliss and contentment. This impressionable period of suffering, followed by miraculous rescue, became the template for the ever-morphing yet consistent thematic expression of my personal story. This early contentment delivered by my initial rescue lasted until the years of puberty and the tyranny of hormones. I didn't feel victimized by my hormones—I probably had never heard the word *hormone*—but I felt betrayed and victimized by the awkwardness of my body, and the horror of body hair that had been downy becoming dark and profuse.

I felt ugly, and I believed the feeling to be an indication of the truth of myself. I could look in the mirror and see ugliness, and I could look inside myself—as best as I knew how—and see the same relentless ugliness. I still wasn't aware of any hidden pleasure in these assessments and feelings, but there was actually a perverse and slightly thrilling feeling of martyrdom. A sense of being right in being wronged has the hidden pleasure of masochism in its makeup.

**Rescue from misery** was the end point in the drama of my misery. In my theater there was no knowledge of causeless peace. Peace only followed—and therefore was a result of—war of some kind. A betrayal of some sort would lead to redemption of some sort. I was involved in the theatrics so fully that initially there was no consciousness of the role I was playing. Even though I would be dismally surprised at an ending of a period of ease or bounty, in my inner theater it had to be that way. How could the prince kiss me awake from the wicked witch's spell if there was no wicked witch?

My drama did not end at that point, but the recognition of my willing participation in my own emotional pain was the death knell for the choice to continue to typecast myself as a victim. What began to unravel was my enjoyment of the drama, along with the willingness to discover how I habitually re-created it. By beginning to tell the truth, it became clear to me that I had to repeatedly replay with specific, painful imagery, the latest point of betrayal. I would have to restimulate my suffering, which was an actual physical pain: a knife in the heart or the gut. And I did this—I could now see—for the morbid entertainment of hurting.

It was easy to assign the role of the wicked witch. Life's reversals provided many victimizers for my role as victim. And the prince with his magic kiss? Oh, that was always the thrilling reward for my suffering. But when I finally saw that I was getting drunk on my own pain, my habit began to lose its hidden appeal. I did—and do—get heartbroken, but my inner theatrics, which had seemed uniquely tragic, were revealed to be unoriginal and banal. I embarrassed myself into sobriety.

**Some years** after this recognition, I discovered how my identity as *someone* was linked to replaying my sad old drama. This discovery helped me see how automatic and even impersonal my particular style of suffering was. Even with that revelatory discovery, it was not until I met Papaji that I even considered the possibility that the entire story might come to an end. It was only in meeting Papaji and by following his instructions that I realized I had been attempting to make the illusion of me—generated by years of playacting—real.

I had assumed that with enough work on my story and my choices, I could make a better story. Yet no matter how much better my story became—and it did become a good story—I was still working it. I had discovered I had been the cause of my addiction to suffering, and now I saw myself as the cause of my happiness. The results were much better, but the work was endless. And it was never enough. There was still never enough love or proof of love, never enough recognition, never enough health, never enough youth. It was all about *me* in the latest incarnation of "good story" with the reversal waiting in the wings, or so I still deeply feared.

**In my late twenties** I had been shocked that I couldn't force myself into the mold of the perfect wife and perfect mother after the novelty of the roles wore off. In my thirties I was shocked that the libertine lifestyle of the 1970s didn't deliver the freedom I longed for. Later I was shocked when meditative experiences of expansion and peace accompanied by profound insight didn't last. I was dismayed that everything I could do or make, however inspiring and wonderful at the time, was destined to always disappear. And when I looked around outside the limited sphere of my own life, I saw the same.

Youth ages, talents wane, possibilities end. Civilizations had flourished and crumbled that I could only identify by exotic names: Phoenicia, Scythia, Inca—all gone. Various empires that had ruled most of their known universes had ended in infamy or obscurity. Legends survived of Arthurian times or of Atlantis, but the truth of the place and the people was gone. Religions had long lost the simplicity of their inspirations, revolutions had ended in becoming what they had fought, people were dying every second.

I finally had to come to terms with the stark truth that I could neither force nor seduce life into giving me what I wanted, much less into having it last forever. I had to grow up. Everything ends. I was in my forties when I finally surrendered to life rather than continuing my absurd and frustrating attempts to control it. I finally, truly, realized that whatever I acquired was bound to change. Nothing stayed the same.

If what I wanted—peace of mind, happiness, love, security— was bound to change, what then? I needed to know what was possible. I had read of yogis and saints who lived in continual states of bliss, but it was hard to relate my situation to theirs. I didn't imagine that I would develop enough yogic powers to maintain any steady state of bliss. Did that mean I was doomed to the perpetual return of misery? I really didn't know what enlightenment meant, but if it meant knowing the truth about life and its real possibilities, I knew I wanted that. I surrendered my ideas about life as well as most of my ideas about myself, and prayed for true understanding. I began the challenge of stopping work on my story.

Working on making a good or even great story is doomed to failure until the story is realized to be *just a story*. Working on illusion does not affect what is real, but it does tend to make the illusion seem more real. However involved an author or reader of a story may be, he or she always has the choice to put the story aside. I finally was ready to at least face that choice. You have that same choice available to you.

This surrender was the preparation for meeting my teacher. When he advised me to find what "doesn't come and go," I knew that everything I could name comes and goes. When he told me, "Only what is changeless is real," my attention quickened. When he told the story of meeting his master, Ramana Maharshi, and asking if Ramana could show him the same gods that he, Papaji, had seen in visions, and of Ramana's replying, "Gods that come and go are useless, find out what is always here," a resonance vibrated within me.

Still, it was a leap of faith to withdraw my attention from those things that were bound to change. I had kept faith that someday I could stabilize the shifting sands of my moods and emotions. They had become more stable, yet unwanted moods still appeared. If I let go of the attention spent on hoping and working for stability, mightn't I lose what I had gained? If I stopped waiting for an experience or an inner event that would never change, would I be giving up my place in line for just such an event?

Papaji would laugh at my concerns. "You are afraid because you still see yourself as separate from reality. You still see yourself as separate from what you long for." His laughter was loving and encouraging, but it was also ruthless. He was not supporting me in generating a better story, or a better role in my story. He was not "empowering" *me*. He was continually pointing out that my *me* only existed in my mind and in the other minds I had enrolled in the illusion. To me his instruction *to stop* initially felt like death; in reality it was life unencumbered by all the stitched-together threads that formed my identity.

Without knowing exactly how to surrender, I was willing to take the plunge. I was willing to stop telling my story, and I now invite you to stop telling yours.

When we are willing for our particular story to end, even momentarily, we discover that what remains is open-ended. Then when or if the story reappears or another one takes its place, stories are recognized to be fodder for deeper inquiry.

Papaji refused the role of rescuer and advised me to stop working on anything, at least for a moment of inquiry. He directed my attention to what was here before my drama, during all dramas, and what remained when each particular drama was finished. He wouldn't accept a role in my familiar, threadbare drama. He brought the curtain down and revealed it all to be a farce. I had experienced "my problem" as a recurring tragic nightmare, but in seeing it as it truly was—fabricated by my thoughts—I began to laugh.

I discovered the healing balm of self-laughter. I recognized the comedic aspect of the tragicomedies we live in our individual mind productions. I laughed at myself in wonder and love as I realized that my comedy is much more life-infused than my tragedy.

**Stories morph** and reappear. The recognition of the change-less, naked ground of silent awareness does not keep stories at bay. Self-recognition simply and profoundly reveals that no story can disrupt silent awareness. Papaji referred to *parabda karma* as the continuation of the story of a particular life. Choices still have consequences, cause and effect are still present, and actions will still be either appropriate or inappropriate. Yet, freshly and surprisingly, silent awareness is revealed to be the core of all new and old versions of anything that appears. The story may evoke extreme emotions, yet it cannot hide what remains at peace.

**In 2005** I discovered that my husband was in love with another woman and had been having an affair with her for the previous three years. The fact that she was also his traveling assistant and student complicated and deepened the shock. Anger, disbelief, and deep hurt flooded through my emotional body. This was an unexpected story of betrayal that shook me in every way. I contributed to the story by giving vent to my anger and indulging my hurt. I screamed at him and threw things. I never wanted to see him again, and I felt hate. The power of disillusionment brought me to my knees. And yet there was also never an absence of love. There was always silence at the core.

By the simple and profound recognition of the ever-present silence, I didn't have to dig out my old rags of victimhood. I didn't have to continually mentally reenact the tragedy and torture myself. I could feel whatever feelings arose and recognize myself as both connected to all those feelings and free of them all. I could stand naked as silence as the weavings of old stories of betrayal and loss appeared and disappeared. Essentially naked, I could meet this story.

We realized that our story as a couple with all its twists and turns now needed to end. We let each other go. We stopped our story, and while we each felt the enormous pain of losing each other, we also felt freedom as the burden of *us* fell away. The emotions that followed were many and complex. There were many tears. I was living through the death of the illusion of my indestructible relationship. It wasn't easy but it was necessary. As much as I cherished him and our relationship, I knew myself as fulfilled and happy even in the grief of losing what I loved.

After a brief but complete separation, we reconciled. The uncontrollable love that had brought us together thirty years earlier brought us together again. But in this reconciliation we came together without needing fulfillment from each other. Thirty years before we had each been seeking fulfillment and either we saw each other as an object necessary for that fulfillment or as an object blocking that fulfillment. We now each realized that the seeds of our betrayal story had been planted in that earlier immaturity and ignorance. And we committed ourselves to deconstructing our mutual roles in this drama.

The story of our subtle and hidden choices to hide from each other and be victimized and extract revenge on each other had to be exposed. Each day we would look deeply into our story. We had to see how we had been at war. The story pointed to where deceit and darkness still needed truth and light. We had to each be willing to take and bear responsibility for our roles. We had to discover hidden justifications and rationalizations for ignoring and denying the dysfunction of our relationship.

It was a humbling and sweetly deepening time. It was humanizing and transcendent at the same time. We would wince at our pettiness, and either laugh or cry at our stupidity as we drew closer to each other as both divine companions and flawed human beings.

Without the reversal of fortune in my marriage, I could never have had the chance to look as deeply as I did at our teaching story of thirty years of love, adventure, hidden needs and hurts, rage, and then release and resolution. I found a deeper redemption in the midst of loss. In the willingness to tell the truth of what was lost, I discovered more fully what was still present.

I'm not happy that it took betrayal to wake up our marriage, just as I am not happy about many of the stories operating in the world. I am happy that we took the opportunity of disillusionment to look into the story and into our hearts. We are both still flawed human beings, and we are in divine relationship.

It is always possible that I am to be blindsided again in my life story with surprises both negative and positive. We all have the capability to ignore what finally must be seen. My teacher cautioned me that vigilance is necessary until the last breath. It is my direct experience that this is so.

This book is not the end of my story or your story, as the multiple stories that our mental, physical, and emotional bodies display will most likely continue for some time. This book can signal the end of how you have been choosing to tell and identify your story as the reality of yourself. You can end your starring role in the story you have named *Me, the Victim* as well as the story *Me, the Hero*. You can choose to disidentify with roles of unnecessary suffering that appear from past dramas of your life. And—most important—you can realize that whatever story is being told is always *just a story*. However identified you find yourself to be in your story, you always have the choice to inquire deeper. Without denying or demeaning your story, you can realize the ground of being it arises in and recognize that ground as the living continual truth of yourself. You can end your identification with your story before death ends it.

Suffering caused by identification with your story as the truth of yourself can end. No more time is needed. Your story is yours certainly, and maybe it is even an important story. Your story is illuminated by the mysterious consciousness that generates and attends it, but still your story is a story. A story has a beginning, a middle, and an end. A story, like a body, has a birth and a death. Inquiring deeply into your story, or into any story, reveals the teaching nature of all stories. Inquiry reveals consciousness recognizing itself in all forms and all versions of all stories. We don't have to be tyrannized by any story that appears in consciousness, even though we may experience deep pain or great joy with particular aspects of any story.

The body has its own story and timeline, which continues until it dies. The stories from the past may show up in memory or dreams or events. Habits and behaviors may or may not continue. The roles of the past may be resurrected and replayed. None of that has any effect on the recognition of yourself as the conscious silent core that is aware of itself in and out of all stories. Suddenly and in time you recognize yourself as both always free of your story as well as the impetus that drove the story to discover its author.

Through cycles and repeating cycles over eons and eons: winning and losing, sleeping and waking, knowing and forgetting, seeing and being blind, hearing and being deaf, intensity and numbness, openhearted and cynical, in plot and subplot, as protagonist and antagonist, hero and villain, tyrant and liberator, extraordinary and ordinary, ornate and simple, told and retold, we can recognize aspects of ourselves in every known or imagined character and situation.

At last we can finally and fully recognize our true self as the silent aware consciousness that all the characters and circumstances occur in.

# CHAPTER 13

# Silent Awareness

Before all, above all, underneath all, and in the midst of all stories, there is silence. Spacious, boundless, and mysterious in its existence, it is always present. We fear utter silence as it represents the state of death and yet long for it as our nightly renewal. It is invisible yet substantial, as it cannot be destroyed. It can be overlooked or covered with the noise of internal and external images and thoughts, but it remains here, after all else has come and gone.

It cannot be learned, since it is the field where all knowledge arises and disappears. One can't acquire silent awareness, but anyone can recognize that awareness itself *is* silent in the depths, no matter how much noise or agitation is present on the surface.

Silent awareness is the changeless subject. All objects appear and disappear in it. Material and subtle forms of every kind, all states of mind, everything we call reality appears in silent awareness. The objects come and go, and silent awareness remains.

Awareness is inherently free of definition, although its name is loosely used to define particular *states* of awareness—transcendent awareness, mundane awareness, subconscious awareness. Silent and conscious, awareness has no need for name or form of even the subtlest kind for its boundaryless existence, yet no name or form can be separate from it.

The discovery that silent awareness is the unchanging presence of one's true identity is momentous beyond measure. All the ways we have defined ourselves disappear in the expansive instant of recognition of changeless, formless, silent presence. We naturally and profoundly rejoice as we recognize that regardless of any name or form, acquisition or loss, positive or negative experience, *this* is always present. *This* is who I am. *This* is who you are.

**It has been said** throughout the ages that the essence of what we realize, when we realize the truth, cannot be spoken. And yet, as human beings with our extraordinary power of language, we must speak. And if we fail in our speaking, if our language comes up short again and again, we fail blissfully. When we fail in using the tools of our evolved intellect to capture the very source of intellect, it is a blessed, humbling failure.

When language is used to attempt to carry the transmission of silence, words can never be enough. Concepts can never be enough. Conceptually understanding what is being said can never be enough. What *is* enough is opening the thinking-processing center of our brains to receptivity. What is then naturally revealed is what is at the ground of the thinking process.

The "I" that we all use to refer to ourselves is the root. The ground, without which there would be no root, is silent awareness. Giving birth to all, receiving all in death, the ground remains both irrevocably inseparable from all and paradoxically free of all. The mother of all Buddhas and all Judases too. The pardon of all sins, the welcome home. Conscious animation of individuality and conscious formlessness simultaneously, it knows itself as one exclusively, and then as all.

**Papaji would respond** to seekers' requests for instructions for realizing the truth by saying, "Keep quiet." These simple words would sometimes strike a mighty blow, and the seeker would be stunned by the revelation of the quiet mind. Sometimes a student would rebel at the words, as they evoked unpleasant memories of being a small child being told to be quiet. Often some time was required for the radical nature of the phrase "Keep quiet" to sink in. He wasn't admonishing his students to stop talking. He was pointing us to our true nature. He was pointing our attention to what is here whether there are thoughts or not. When he said, "Keep quiet," he was pointing to the silent awareness that is who one is. He was giving instructions to be who you are.

When it did sink in, laughter was usually the immediate result.

Laughter often accompanied by tears of joy. How close it has always been! As Papaji would point out, "Closer than the breath, closer than the heartbeat."

Later, when thoughts came barging back in, thoughts like "I got it. My mind stopped. My God, I never knew this could happen," Papaji would smile or laugh and say, "Very good, very good. Now keep still." If the seeker was truly earnest or at least recognized that there was an opportunity like none before, he or she would keep quiet. Keep quiet and listen. Papaji's teachings were direct and simple. "Find out what is changeless. Discover what doesn't come and go. Stop your searching. Find out who you are."

To all the questions of *how* and *why* and *when*, Papaji would direct the questioner back to silence. He called silence the substratum. To some it seemed that the goal was to simply not speak or not think. Later it became clear that the point of allowing the thoughts to return to the substratum, the point of keeping quiet, is to realize that it is silence itself that is always here. Thoughts or no thoughts, silence remains, silence which is overflowing with the fullness of being, being conscious of itself. If bliss appears or if despair appears, silent awareness remains the unmoving substratum.

**Papaji never wanted** us to learn about silence; he wasn't offering a class in self-awareness. He was always encouraging us to be willing to be absolutely still and then to discover for ourselves what that stillness is.

Often long-term meditators would come to him, serious seek-ers who had practiced meditation for years, many in long retreats with hours of sitting in meditation. He was happy to see them, but he was not impressed with their history of practice. While he would often allow his mind to fall into deep, thoughtless pres-ence, the silence he pointed to couldn't be acquired or practiced. He would say that the true meditation was *dhyana,* which he translated as "no mind." Too often practicing only more firmly roots the concept of a practitioner, someone who is getting closer to some future attainment.

Papaji made no distinction between new seekers and those who had been on the path for decades. "Keep still, find out who you are. Who is practicing? Who is new on the path?"

All who were not overly identified with themselves as "some-one who . . ." could experience their mind stopped in its tracks. They could then drink deeply of the transmission that he offered, and whether their practices continued or not, they tasted the truth of themselves as silence. Beyond and before all practice, unchanging in the midst of all religions and belief systems is silent awareness.

We are all in the habit of practicing. Most of us practice being the person we think we are, or who we think we should be. On any given day, how much time is spent internally repeating defi-nitions of ourselves? "I am hopelessly stupid," or "I am the most intelligent person I know." After a bad day perhaps "I am doomed to be unhappy," or after an exceptionally good day, "I am going to be happy all the days of my life." How many hours are spent imagining what our past could have been or what our future may be? We have internal images of ourselves that we judge both positively and negatively. As we practice being who we think we are, we are watching and hearing a version of our life inside our minds, and generally we are so used to our version that we take it to be reality.

We may call our time on the meditation cushion "our practice," but that time is—in the best "practices"—when our normal, day-to-day practicing actually stops. For twenty minutes or an hour we don't have to remember who or how we should be; we don't have to practice a past or a future. We can stop. Those who have had this experience want more, but few realize that more is already here as the ground that all our histories, and *shoulds*, and *wills*, and *mights* sprout on. It is here each moment, not just the time spent on our cushions. And there is always more of it when we are willing to stop our habitual practices and simply be still.

This discovery is instantly fulfilling, and an ongoing unfolding mystery. It is a discovery of oneself, unburdened by any idea of oneself. Oneself unburdened by thoughts of oneself, and needing nothing for the release of that burden. Oneself before ignorance or enlightenment, before name or gender or history, and after all naming, and in the midst of any appearance of gender and history. Oneself as indefinable and as the one found in the definition of all things. Only silent awareness doesn't come and go. Only silent awareness is found in all that does come and go.

———————

Papaji was a householder. He had a job and a family. He had to spend time speaking. One of the benefits of his being a householder is that he had to find the reality of absolute silence within the interplay of relative noise and relative silence. It is a benefit to us that he made this discovery.

One of the most important moments in my time with Papaji was a day when he took us to the market in Haridwar. Indian markets, similar to markets everywhere, are noisy places. They are centers of activity with all types of people shouting or singing or begging people to buy their goods. Added to the noise and the smells was the enervating heat of midday.

Earlier that morning we had been sitting peacefully in his small rooms by the river. While at the hot market I had thoughts of wanting to be back in the peace of his rooms with the cooling breeze of the river and the only sound being the *whap, whap* of the ceiling fan. After internally complaining for a moment or two, I looked up and happened to catch his eye. With startling clarity I seemed to hear him say, "Here too." In wonder and bliss, the silence underneath the noise was suddenly obvious. "Underneath the noise" is not precisely correct, but at the time it appeared that way. Later I realized that whatever the noise level, I am here also, and I am silence itself.

Whether listening to Papaji deliver a dharma discourse, hearing him tell a teaching story or some story from his earlier life, going shopping with him for vegetables for the evening meal, or sitting simply in his rooms, each moment was an invitation to silence. Each word was pointing back to and bringing the news of its silent origin.

Papaji would sometimes spend time with a student carefully directing him to follow a thought back into the empty, open space it had come from. He would ask the student to choose any thought and speak it out loud. The student might respond, "I can't stop my thoughts." Then Papaji would direct, "Follow that thought all the way back from whence it came. First the 'I' falls back, then the 'can't,' then the 'stop,' then the 'my,' then the 'thoughts' . . . What is left now?"

In the luminous open mind, free of the thought that disappeared when followed back rather than chased forward into the ten thousand thoughts, the student's face would be filled with wonder.

Papaji would finish with: "Now, tell me, who are you?"

The result of this invitation to silence is not somber by any means. With Papaji there was often uproarious laughter. Sometimes there would be no words spoken for hours, and sometimes there would be lively conversation. The conversation had no prescribed boundaries; it could be about the deepest spiritual concerns or the upcoming cricket match. It could be a discussion of train schedules, the politics of India, or of the growing numbers of seekers who were finding him. Whatever the conversation, or lack of conversation, whether there was laughter or simple quiet reflection, there was always an overflowing of love.

This abundant love is the hidden treasure that the quiet mind reveals. It doesn't need to be talked about, and it is natural to experience and share it. Love isn't taught. It is discovered.

In the willingness to keep quiet, deeper yielding to silent, aware love is always available. If old habits of grasping and controlling arise, the simple, profoundly effective "Keep quiet" allows an always fresh discovery of the ever-present silent awareness that *is* love. Finally there is a falling so fully into silence that there can be no doubt that it is *silent-aware-love* that you are.

True, absolute silence and true, absolute love are not different. Absolute silent awareness overflows with simple, fulfilled absolute love. Objects—people, nature, emotions—may or may not appear. Objects are not needed and they are welcomed.

The joy of this full silence is uncaused and unlimited. Always here, always discovering itself. It is the treasure, and it is hidden only when we refuse to keep quiet and find out who we are.

**Spotlessness and filth** are equally pure as silent awareness.

Thrills of wonder and stillness of deep sleep are equally included in silent awareness.

Destroyer of all paradox, solvent of differences, allowing all, it reigns supreme by doing nothing. Aware of sublime and subtle states, aware of unspeakable horrors, it welcomes equally the mundane and the profound.

Lover of love, greeter of hate, silently observing what is formed of its substance. Universes of infinite movement formed of itself, unmoving. Brahman, Atman, Soul, you, me, we, they, all, and none. Only it recognizes itself.

In a transparent moment of quiet, in the passion of war, in the lover's surrender, in the resistance of *no*, silent awareness knows itself. In the saint, the killer, the killed; in the worshipped and the reviled, the chased and the caught, it recognizes itself.

In the dawning of *me*, in the recognition of *other*, in meeting *the end*, silent awareness always—whatever the direction and whatever the way—remains the same.

Throughout all obscuration and all revelation, throughout all ignorance and all knowing, silent awareness: generator of all remains free of all.

In music of the spheres and grating sounds of discord, silent awareness is equally present. In deepest grief and exultant ecstasy, silent awareness remains the same.

Within the rulers of the world and the downtrodden equally. The ocean with all its waves and the shore. The meeting place of ocean and shore equally.

At every moment, in every state, in all forms of conscious, unconscious, subconscious, and supraconscious, silent awareness is unmovingly present.

The attractor and the repelled, the seeker and the oblivious. In all distinctions, in all equalizations too. Both known and unknown, spoken and unspeakable, eternally realized and eternally uncapturable.

Immeasurable and yet smallest of the small, having no limits even of limitlessness. Only it recognizes itself, always freshly, and anciently too.

Infusing and seeing the best and the worst. Expressed by art and the artless. Including itself in all.

Recognize yourself as it. Speak it if you can. Discover limits if possible. Report to yourself all of it, your exploration of it as your own self.

# ACKNOWLEDGMENTS

Ongoing gratitude for all those who read and made suggestions for the improvement of this book. Especially: Eli, Roslyn and Bruce Moore, Harriet Brittain, Barbara Denempont, and Manju Lyn Bazzell.

Thanks to Ed and Deb Shapiro for their openhearted full support. They introduced me to the literary agent David Nelson of Waterside Productions, who was the first one to strongly encourage me to write this book and has been with me all the way.